ON PURGATORY

De Controversiis

On Purgatory

St. Robert Bellarmine, S.J.
Doctor of the Church

Translated from the Latin by
Ryan Grant

MEDIATRIX PRESS

MMXVII

ISBN: 978-1-953746-61-0

© Ryan Grant, 2017
All Rights reserved. No part of this work may be reproduced without the express permission of the publisher, except for educational purposes of a Church, reviews, or citations.

Cover art: *Purgatory*, by Annibale Carraci

Mediatrix Press
607 E. 6th Ave Ste. 230
Post Falls, ID 83854
http://www.mediatrixpress.com

TABLE OF CONTENTS

PREFACE. 1

BOOK I
    ON THE EXISTENCE OF PURGATORY

CHAPTER I
    On the word "Purgatory". 5

CHAPTER II
    On the errors concerning Purgatory. 7

CHAPTER III
    Purgatory is proven from the scriptures of the Old Testament. 13

CHAPTER IV
    Purgatory is proven from the New Testament. . . . 26

CHAPTER V
    1 Corinthians 3:15. 31

CHAPTER VI
    1 Corinthians 15:29. 54

CHAPTER VII
    Matthew 5:25 and Luke 12:58. 62

CHAPTER VIII
    Matthew 5:22, Luke 16:9, Luke 23:42, Acts 2:24 and Philippians 2:10. 71

CHAPTER IX
    Purgatory is asserted in the testimonies of Councils 77

CHAPTER X
    Purgatory is asserted in the testimonies of the Greek and Latin Fathers......................... 83

CHAPTER XI
    The same is asserted from reason. 95

CHAPTER XII
    Arguments from the Scriptures are answered. .. 105

CHAPTER XIII
    Objections from the Fathers are answered. 112

CHAPTER XIV
    Answer to objections raised from reason. 118

CHAPTER XV
    The Confession of Purgatory pertains to the Catholic faith..................................... 128

BOOK II
    ON THE CIRCUMSTANCES OF PURGATORY

CHAPTER I
    On the persons for whom Purgatory is suited. . 139

CHAPTER II
In Purgatory, souls can neither gain merit nor sin 148

CHAPTER III
Objections are answered. 153

CHAPTER IV
The souls in Purgatory are certain about their eternal salvation. 162

CHAPTER V
Objections made from the prayers of the Church are answered. 171

CHAPTER VI
On the place of Purgatory. 176

CHAPTER VII
Whether after this life, there is some place for just souls apart from Heaven and Purgatory. 184

CHAPTER VIII
Whether souls of the dead might avail to leave their receptacles. 186

CHAPTER IX
On the time in which Purgatory endures. 196

CHAPTER X
What kind of punishment is in Purgatory? 202

CHAPTER XI
The fire of Purgatory is corporeal. 204

CHAPTER XII
It cannot be known how corporeal fire burns souls 206

CHAPTER XIII
Whether souls in Purgatory are tortured by demons 207

CHAPTER XIV
On the gravity of punishments. 208

CHAPTER XV
The suffrage of the Church benefits the dead. . 213

CHAPTER XVI
How many kinds of suffrage are there? 221

CHAPTER XVII
Who can assist souls. 224

CHAPTER XVIII
Who benefits from suffrage? 225

CHAPTER XIX
On funerals. 232

Preface of the Author

ITHERTO we have made our dissertation on the part of the Church which is on earth: Now we must dispute on that which abides within the earth; then we will dispute lastly on that part of the Church which reigns in heaven; and because the faithful who have already died but are not yet among the blessed abide within the earth, although their body and soul are in different places, so first we will speak about the place of souls, secondly on the place of the bodies, that is, on burial.

But before we come to the questions, we must preface three things. 1) What we understand in this place by the name of Purgatory; 2) What errors there are about Purgatory; 3) In what order this disputation should be explained.

Moreover, there are many that have written on Purgatory. John Fisher of Rochester against the articles of Luther; John Eck (lib. 4 *de Purgatorio*); John Bunderius in his *Compendium*, tit. 18; Joannes Garetius (libro de oratione pro defunctis); Jacobus Latomus in explicatione arctic. sexti Lovaniensium; Jodocus Clichtovaeus in libro de Purgatorio; Bernard Lutzenburg, lib. unico de Purgatorio; Alphonsus de Castro, *verbo Purgatorium*; Martin Persius Aiala de traditionibus; Claudius Coussord contra Waldenses; Cajetan tomo 1. tract. 2, 3, et 24; Francis Orantius, libro 4 de locis Catholicis; Hugo Etherianus de regressu animarum ab inferis; Catharinus libro de veritate Purgatorii.

BOOK I
ON THE EXISTENCE OF PURGATORY

CHAPTER I
On the word "Purgatory"

N Scripture we find three passages to which a purgation of sinners is attributed, and they can be called purgatories. 1) Christ himself, about whom Hebrews 1:3 says: "making purgation for sinners." and John 1:29, "Behold the lamb of God, behold he who takes away the sins of the world." Yet, we do not say this is about Purgatory, both because Christ is not usually called a "Purgatory" and because it is beyond controversy that he is the one who purges sins.

2) The tribulations of this life, on which it seems Malachi must be understood literally, "He is like a refining fire, and the fuller's herb; he will sit refining and cleansing the silver, and he will purge the sons of Levi and will refine them just like gold and silver." (Malachi 3:2-3). For, as St. Jerome rightly explains, here it is a question of the tribulation which precedes the day of judgment to purge the sins of the faithful, and John 15:2 says, "Every vine not bearing fruit will be cut down and every one that bears fruit, he will cleanse that it should offer the fruit." Yet we do not say this is about Purgatory, both because it is beyond controversy and also because the tribulation of this life is not always a purgatory. For there are many just men that are afflicted, not that they be purged, but that they should be cultivated and proved according to the saying of Sirach 27:6, "The furnace proves vessels of clay, just as

tribulation the just man." And many unjust are afflicted, not that they be purged, but that they should begin to taste the punishments of damnation.

Therefore, 3) Purgatory is called a certain place in which, like a prison, souls which were not fully purged here on earth are purged after this life, that so purged they may undoubtedly avail to enter heaven, in which nothing tainted will enter. On this is the whole controversy.

CHAPTER II
On the Errors Concerning Purgatory

HERE were many errors on Purgatory which contradict each other. First of all, are those who were against Purgatory. It seems that the heretic Aërius was such, as Epiphanius (*haer.* 75), and Augustine (*haer.* 53) witness since he taught that one must not pray for the dead. Hence it follows, that they either do not need prayers or cannot be helped, and both of these oppose Purgatory, at least in the mode of its existence which is posited by the Church.

Moreover, the Waldensians denied Purgatory, as Guido the Carmelite relates (*Summa de haereticis*) as well as St. Antoninus (4 *parte*, tit. II, cap. 7, §2, *summae Theologiae*).

The Apostolics taught the same thing, as St. Bernard relates (serm. 66 in *Cantica*) and perhaps the Waldensians are the offspring of the Apostolics; for they agree in the errors that are attributed to them and they were near to each other in time. The sect of the Waldensians arose around 1160 AD, according to the *Chronicle* of Trithemius, or around 1170 according to Guido in his *summa* (c. 1), and Reynerius, who lived three hundred years ago, and one can see his testimony at the end of the book of Claudius Cussordius against the Waldensians. Moreover, the Apostolics are a little earlier, since they began in the times of St. Bernard, who died in the year 1153. That the Waldensians also wanted to be called Apostolics, because they would follow the poverty of the Apostles, is manifest from their history, related by Aemilius (lib. 6 *de gestis*

Francorum), and the Abbot of Ursburg in his *Chronicle* for the year 1212.

Henry and Peter Bruis taught the same thing with the Waldensians in the same time, against whom St. Bernard (epist. 240), and Peter the Cluniac (*in epistola ad omnes Episcopos*) wrote.

Later, the Albigensians taught the same thing, and they not only denied Purgatory, but also abolished hell, as St. Antoninus witnesses (4 p.t. II, c. 7, §5).

Bernard of Lutzenburg, in the preface to his book on Purgatory, attributes the same thing to the followers of Wycliffe and Hus, but perhaps falsely, since neither the Council of Constance nor Thomas Waldens attribute any such thing to them, while Aeneas Sylvius, who also numbered this among the errors of the Hussites in his book on the origin of the Bohemians, (chapter 35), seems to have confused Hussites with Waldensians.

The same is attributed to the Armenians and the Greeks by Guido the Carmelite in his *Summa de Haereticis*, and although the Greeks themselves, at the Council of Ferrara (sess. 1), affirmed that they do not deny Purgatory, but only the fire, and think that Purgatory is a dark place and full of labors, still it is credible that the Greeks were at least suspect of this heresy. St. Thomas, in his work *Against the Errors of the Greeks* also refuted this error, and proves that there is a Purgatory, and in the last session of the Council of Florence, the same error was condemned. Nevertheless, in that Council only the errors of the Greeks were condemned, or at least those in which the Greeks were suspect.

At length, Luther and all of his posterity, although divided into different sects, nevertheless agree to abolish

Ch. II: Errors about Purgatory 9

Purgatory, although Luther himself was very different. For 1) He plainly admitted Purgatory in a Catholic sense in the Leipzig debate, which is still extant: "I, who firmly believe, nay more dare to say that there is a Purgatory, I am easily persuaded that mention is made of it in Scripture."

The next error does admit Purgatory, but it is mixed with many errors. The first error was that Purgatory cannot be proven from Scripture. The second, that it is not certain that the souls in Purgatory will attain salvation. The third error, is that souls in Purgatory can merit or lose merit. The fourth, that souls in Purgatory sin without pause, while they abhor punishment and seek rest. Fifth, that the souls which are freed by the suffrage of the Church are less happy than if they had made satisfaction by themselves. These five are contained in various articles condemned by Leo, at the end.

The last error simply abolishes Purgatory in regard to suffrage for the dead, and asserts there is no Purgatory after this life, but only in life and in death; for the horror and the punishment of death itself purges if anything remains which must be purged. Luther so taught in his book *On the Abrogation of private Mass*, where he says it is better to deny the whole of Purgatory than to believe the reference of St. Gregory to apparitions of souls begging for suffrage, and in the book to the Waldensians, *de Eucharistia*: "I also approve of everything [you have said] that when you deny Purgatory, you also deny Masses, vigils, monks, monasteries and whatever is erected by this cheat."

All the heretics of this time follow the last position. The rigid Lutherans, such as the Centuriators (*Cent.*, I, lib. 2, cap. 4, col. 460; Cent. 4, cap. 4, col. 304), soft Lutherans, as Melanchthon relates (*in locis ca. de satisfactione*), and Brenz in the Wurtemberg Confession, in the chapter *de Purgatorio*. Likewise, the Zwinglians, as Cochleus relates in the acts of Luther for the year 1526, and Bernard Ochinus in his *Dialogo de Purgatorio*, and Calvin in the *Institutes* (lib. 3, ca. 5, §6), where he says that Purgatory is a deadly fiction of Satan which makes void the cross of Christ, because it inflicts an insupportable contumely on the mercy of God, which undermines and overturns our faith. Peter Martyr, in chapter 3 of 1 Cor. 2, says two things. First, whether there is or is not a Purgatory it is certainly not a dogma of faith. Second, he says it is not probable that Purgatory exists. And then the Trinitarian Anabaptists, in chapter 1 of book 2 from those they recently published in the year 1567, say Luther laid the foundation of the Reformation of the Church when he abolished Purgatory, Masses and like things. The foundation of all the Lutherans is that they abolish satisfaction and the distinction of mortal and venial sin, for after they have posited that foundation, it necessarily follows that there is no Purgatory.

Moreover, they are not lacking, who would so prove Purgatory that they acknowledge no penalties but the purgatories after this life. Origen so thought that it was promised to all impious men and demons that at length they would be saved, as Epiphanius relates in his epistle to John of Jerusalem, and Augustine (*de Civitate Dei*, lib. 2, ca. 17), where he adds the opinion of others who acknowledged, not indeed the penalties of demons, but those of all men to be only purgatories. He also says in the same work, book 21, ca. 13, that the same opinion was that of the Platonists: clearly there is no punishment after this

Ch. II: Errors about Purgatory

life but purgatory, and it was clear from those verses of Virgil in the *Aeneid*:

Blunt not the beams of heav'n and edge of day.
From this coarse mixture of terrestrial parts,
Desire and fear by turns possess their hearts,
And grief, and joy; nor can the groveling mind,
In the dark dungeon of the limbs confin'd,
Assert the native skies, or own its heav'nly kind:
Nor death itself can wholly wash their stains.[1]

Although we read another thing in the works of Plato, for in the *Phaedo* as well as in the *Gorgias*, there are three kinds of men who are called to judgment after death. One of these, who lived piously and justly, he says are immediately transferred to the islands of the blessed. The second of these, who committed curable sins, he asserts are punished for a time, until the wickedness is cleansed from them. The third of these, who committed incurable sins, he says are cast into hell to be punished forever, whose punishments benefitted them nothing, but still benefit as an example to others, and Virgil is also not silent about it, for he says:

And bound with burning wires, on spokes of wheels are hung

---

[1] *Quin et supremo cum lumine vita reliquit,*
Non tamen malum miseris, nec funditus omnes
Corporea excedunt pestes, penitusque necesse est
Multa diu concreta modis inolescere miris,
Ergo exercentur poenis, veterumque malorum
Supplicia expendunt, etc. (lib. 6).

Unhappy Theseus, doom'd for ever there,
Is fix'd by fate on his eternal chair;
And wretched Phlegyas warns the world with cries
(Could warning make the world more just or wise):
'Learn righteousness, and dread th' avenging deities.'[2]

And that is sufficient for these.

The whole disputation is contained in ten headings. 1) We will show there is a Purgatory; 2) That it is held by faith; 3) To what persons it is fitting, whether the just, or all sinners, or only certain ones; 4) On the state of those who are in Purgatory, whether they are certain of salvation; 5) They can neither merit nor lose merit; 6) On the place of Purgatory; 7) On the time in which it endures; 8) On the punishment itself, what kind it might be and upon whom it is inflicted; 9) On the remedy for punishment; 10) On the burial of bodies.

---

[2] *Sedet, aeternumque sedebit*
Infelix Theseus Phlegiasque miserrimus, omnes
Admonet et magna testatur voce per umbras.
Discite iustitiam moniti, et non temnere divos.

CHAPTER III
Purgatory is Proven from the Scriptures of the Old Testament

HEREFORE, we will prove that there is a Purgatory by five types of arguments. We will bring forward firstly the Scriptures of the Old Testament. Secondly, the Scriptures of the New Testament. Thirdly Councils. Fourthly the Fathers. Fifthly reasons, and then at length we will answer the opposing arguments. The first passage is contained in 2 Maccabees 12, where after the Scripture says that Judas Machabaeus sent 12,000 silver drachmas to Jerusalem for sacrifices to be offered for the dead, it adds: "Therefore it is a holy and beneficial thought to pray for the dead, that their sins would be forgiven."

Hence it follows: 1) After this life the dead can have their sins forgiven and so there is Purgatory. 2) The sacrifices and prayers of the living benefit the dead. 3) Not all the remnants of sins are expiated in death, as Luther says, since those for whom he commanded prayers to be offered died a violent death, and for religion; nevertheless Judas still believed they were not fully cleansed; 4) a man can die in a holy and pious manner and still have some debt to pay, either on account of venial sins that were not remitted in this life or on account of incomplete satisfaction for mortal sins that were forgiven, as the Scripture says about all those for whose sins Judas commanded prayers to be offered, when he obtained their rest by piety; 5) This is de fide.

To this passage our adversaries respond in several ways. *First*, they say this book is not canonical since the author himself seeks forgiveness if he has erred in anything. "Therefore," Brenz says, "pardon is at length his because he erred when he praised patronage for the dead."

Secondly, at least this part (verse 44) cannot be canonical (thinking about the resurrection in a holy and pious manner, for unless those who fell hoped that they would rise from the dead, it seems vain and superfluous to pray for the dead), for it contains a discovered error, namely that souls die and rise again with the bodies, otherwise it would not be vain and superfluous to pray for the dead, even if they would not rise again. Ochinus adds, from this very clause purgatory can be abolished, for if there were a purgatory, but no resurrection of the dead, still it would not be vain to pray for the dead because the prayer would benefit them unto liberation from the punishments of Purgatory.

Thirdly, because that conclusion: "Therefore, the thought is holy and beneficial, etc." does not seem to fit the historian, and perhaps it was some marginal annotation and from there was violently intruded into the text.

Fourthly, because no mention is made in this Scripture of purgatory, but only of the resurrection. It is said that Judas commanded them to pray for the dead while thinking about the resurrection in a holy and pious manner.

Fifthly, because Judas commanded sacrifices and prayers be offered for those whom it is certain died in mortal sin, since we have in the same place that certain things from votive offerings of idols were found under the tunics of those that were slain, which they took against the

Ch. III: Purgatory proven from the Old Testament

express prohibition of Deuteronomy 7: "They found," it says, "under the tunics of the slain the votive offerings of idols, of Jamnia, which the law forbade to the Jews." The fact was made manifest to all, and this is why they came to ruin, therefore what Judas did was either superstitious, or they did not pray so as to help their souls, but merely to console themselves.

Sixthly, because it does not follow that because prayer and sacrifice was made for the dead that therefore they were in Purgatory; those they were praying for could have been in hell, and those that prayed could have offered prayer and sacrifice so as to show their feelings of respect and remembrance toward them, and to console themselves.

Seventhly, because that Scripture does not advance some law or decree, but merely the example of one man, we are not held to imitate it, since by no means can we imitate all the examples of the Scriptures. Nor does the fact that Judas' example is praised in this passage counter this argument, since in the same book the example of Razias is praised, who killed himself (2 Macc. 14:42).

I say to the *first*, the book of Maccabees is not canonical with the Jews, but it is with the Christians. Accordingly, the universal Church reads this book in Mass and read it in former times, as is clear from the epistle of Peter of Cluny against the Petrobrusians, notwithstanding that it was forbidden in the third Council of Carthage (c. 47) for any book to be read in the Church under the name of the divine books unless they were canonical. Besides, the same canon of that Council numbers the book of Maccabees among the divine books, as well as the epistle of Innocent I to Exuperius, and from the fathers, St. Augustine in his *de Civitate Dei*, lib. 18, ch. 36, where he says: "The books of the Maccabees are not held for canonical by the Jews, but by the Church."

From such testimonies that most impudent lie of Ochinus is refuted, who, in his dialogue on Purgatory, says: "They are apocryphal, from Laodicea and manifested in an African Council, and out of all the sacred doctors who enumerated the catalog of the Sacred books, they make no mention of Maccabees." Anyone that has read the Third Council of Carthage, which Ochinus calls "an African Council" will know how openly he lies, and besides this, Pope Innocent I in the place we cited, as well as St. Augustine in book 2 of *de doctrina Christiana*, Gelasius in the decree of the canonical books which he published in a Council of seventy Bishops; Isidore in book 6 *etymolog.* c. 1, and other fathers in the places we cited in *de Verbo Dei*, lib. 1 cap. 15.

Peter Martyr responds (on 1 Corinthians, c. 3) citing Augustine, that the Church itself received this book into the Canon, not of those books which avail to confirm doctrines, but of those which avail for the building up of morals, and he proves it because Augustine, in book 2 against the epistle of Gaudentius, c. 23, says this book is not of equal authority with the law, the prophets, and the Psalms, but it was still useful if read soberly. Likewise, Cyprian says in his exposition of the Creed that these books do not avail to prove doctrines.

But the Pseudomartyr is deceitful in his use of St. Augustine, since the holy doctor so thought this book availed to confirm dogmas that in book 1, ch. 1 *de Cura pro Mortuis*, he seeks his argument from this book alone to prove that one must pray for the dead and that it is a dogma of faith. He teaches the same when in his book *de*

Ch. III: Purgatory proven from the Old Testament 17

haeresibus, c. 52, he places Aërius in the number of the heretics because he denied that prayers could be made for the dead. In his book against Gaudentius, c. 23, he does not say that the books of the Maccabees are not equal to the Psalms, the Law and the Prophets in the Church, but among the Jews: "And truly the Jews do not hold this Scripture, which is called of the Maccabees, as the Law, and the Prophets and the Psalms, but it has been received by the Church and not without profit, if it is soberly read and listened to." From this the typical trickery of Peter Martyr is apparent. Moreover, when Augustine says it ought to be soberly read, he does not mean because there are some errors in this book, but because there are some examples related such as some who killed themselves, and they must not be imitated; in this way even Genesis must be soberly read, lest we might think Judah the Patriarch, who committed incest, must be imitated.

Moreover, the same Peter Martyr was deceived when he adduced Cyprian in place of Ruffinus; that explanation of the Creed is not from Cyprian but Ruffinus, as is clear from the preface, where the author indicates that he is from Aquileia and was baptized as well as educated there, and in the same place he calls to mind the heretic Photinus, who was a hundred years later than Cyprian, and where he enumerates the sacred books, he calls to mind the names of Donatus, Manichaeus, Arius, Eunomius and other heretics who arose after the death of Cyprian. Nor should it be a surprise if Ruffinus did not think these books were canonical, since the books of the Maccabees are from that number over which there was uncertainty for a time even among Catholics, and later they were nevertheless received by the universal Church as truly canonical.

To the first proof I say, the author does not seek pardon for errors but for his style, in the same way that St. Paul excuses himself for inexperience in discourse.

To the *second* I say that the teaching of this book would appear inept, because it misses that among the Jews it was customary at that time to hold that on the resurrection and that on the immortality of souls as the same question, although they are really distinct. For among the Jews, those who denied one, denied the other, *as* the Sadducees, and those who affirmed one also affirmed the other, *as* the Pharisees, as is clear from Acts 23:8. And not without reason, for since the rational soul is the true form of the body, and hence a true part of man, it does not have the appearance of truth that God meant for the soul to live perpetually without the body. Hence, the Lord in Matthew 22:32 proved the resurrection to the Sadducees by using the testimony of Scripture: "I am the God of Abraham, Isaac and Jacob," and he added, "God is not God of the dead, but of the living," from which he meant to argue that the dead rise again.

But this argument concludes nothing unless it is presupposed that the question on the immortality of souls and that on the resurrection of bodies were received for one and the same, for otherwise the consequence can be denied. For God will be God of the living even if the dead do not rise, inasmuch as the souls themselves live. With the same reasoning, the Apostle says, "What good is it if the dead do not rise again? Let us eat, and drink for tomorrow we will die" (1 Cor. 15:32); unless he presupposes that souls are mortal, if bodies do not rise again, he concludes nothing. For if the soul is immortal, even if the bodies do not rise again, it is very beneficial to

Ch. III: Purgatory proven from the Old Testament

fast and to live well, because it is beneficial to acquire the glory of the soul. Therefore, the Scripture of the book of Maccabees speaks altogether in the same mode, in which here St. Paul speaks, and he presupposes the same thing. He means to say, if the dead do not rise, then it follows that souls are mortal and hence it is superfluous and vain to pray for the dead, unless one were to hope in the resurrection.

To the *third*, I say the adverb "therefore", (*ergo*) is not in the Greek text, for we so read: "ει τ' ἐμβλέπον τοις μετ' εὐσεβείαν κοιμωμένοις κάλλισον ἀποκείμενον καριςῆριον, ὀσια καί εὐσεβης ἡ ἐπίνοια, οθεν περὶ τῶν τεθνηκοτων τὸν ἐξιλασμὸν ἐποιήσατο, τῆς ἁμαρτίας ἀπολυθ ναι, this is: "Then considering, that the best grace is reserved to those who fell asleep in godliness, which was a holy and pious consideration, for that reason he made expiation for the dead, that they would be freed from sin." Nevertheless, the sense is altogether the same. The Latin reading cannot be rejected unless one were also to reject the Greek. Nor is it unusual for historians sometimes to gather something from events and deeds which pertains to imitation and good morals.

To the *fourth* I say, it is not necessary for there to have been express mention of purgatory, since it is gathered clearly enough from the events which are contained there. For we are not contending about the name, but about the reality. Nor indeed when it is said that Judas bid prayer to be made for the dead, thinking well and religiously about the resurrection, would the sense be that he commanded them to pray for the dead so that they would rise; rather, the sense is that when Judas thought religiously about the future resurrection, and hence souls being immortal, and he feared lest the souls of his slain soldiers, on account of some sin, would be punished in another age, so he commanded prayer and sacrifice to be made for them so that they would be freed from sins as it is expressed at the end of the chapter.

To *the fifth* I say, their sin was either venial, since perhaps they were ignorant of the prohibition of the law, and did not receive those votives in order to honor idols, but only from the lust to enrich themselves, which can be venial; or certainly if it was a mortal sin, those soldiers were sorrowful for their sin at the moment of death, and it was remitted them as to guilt, according to the saying of Psalm 77(78):34, "When he killed them, they sought him and they turned back"; or at least Judas Machabaeus so thought, otherwise the Scripture would not have said he considered those who fell asleep in godliness to have the best grace reserved for them. I add lastly, at least their state was uncertain, and for that reason it was lawful to pray for them, even if they were damned.

To *the sixth* I say, our consequent is not: They prayed for them therefore they were in Purgatory; rather they prayed for certain dead mean, therefore they thought it could be the case that they were in purgatory, or, that prayer for the sins of the dead is praised in Scripture, therefore there is a Purgatory in another life; for otherwise they made their prayer in vain and the Scripture erred in praising a prayer of this sort. Nevertheless, in this passage prayer for the expiation of sins is praised, and is clearly shown not to have been for human affection; it is clear for two reasons: a) the occasion of this prayer was the sin of those men that had died on whom pagan votive offerings had been found under their clothes, as the history says; b) it is expressly said that Judas sent 12,000 drachmas for sacrifice to be offered for the sins of the dead, and below, that it is so that their sins might be forgiven. Add that if there were no Purgatory, it would indeed be permitted to weep so as to show human affection, but not likewise to pray; to what end would one offer prayer for those who either do not need it, or whom it cannot help?

To the seventh, I say the argument is not taken from the example of one man but partly from the ancient and solemn rite of the Church of the Old Testament and partly from the infallible testimony of Sacred Scripture. That this was a solemn rite of the Old Testament Church is proven when it is said in this passage: "All those who were with Juda turned to prayers," and then: "he took up a collection," *i.e.* each man gave something, a great deal of money was collected, and sent by Juda in the name of all of them to Jerusalem, for sacrifices for the dead; and this indeed is a great argument; but what is greater, establishing the Catholic faith, is what is taken from the words of Scripture praising the prayer made on behalf of the sins of the dead as holy, pious and religious. Next, the instance in regard to the praise of Razias, who killed himself, does not avail, for as St. Augustine shows (lib. 2 *contra epistolam Gaudentii*, cap. 23), Razias is praised because he acted courageously and bravely, not piously and with holiness, or, if they would have it that the deed is approved by the author of this book, it must rather be said that Razias had a peculiar inspiration and precept of God to do this just as Samson had (as Augustine witnesses, *de Civitate Dei*, lib. 1 cap. 21) than that this author could err.

Apart from this passage there are certain others which only furnish probable arguments, which nevertheless the holy Fathers have used. Therefore, we will briefly note them here.

The second passage is Tobias 4:18, "Lay out your bread and wine upon the burial of a just man and do not eat or drink of them with sinners." There can be no other sense than that which the exegetes hand down in common, namely: prepare dinner and call the faithful poor so that they, after they have received an alms, might pray for the soul of the dead man. For hence that custom was born, which was once in the Church, and still exists, that the kin of the deceased should have a dinner and also send food and drink to the poor and religious, so that they would pray for the soul of the dead. St. John Chrysostom asks: "Why do you call the poor together after the death of your own? Why do you beg the priests to pray for them?" (Hom. 32 in Matt.). The commentary of Munster does not have any validity, which interprets tombs to be the mouths of the righteous poor because it is written in Psalm 5:11, "their throat is an open sepulcher," meaning, place your bread in the mouth of the just so that they might not die of hunger. For this explanation is false. *Firstly*, because no scripture calls the mouth of the just a tomb, but only the mouth of the sinner, from where they exhale the stench of their vices. *Secondly*, because Tobias commended the living poor in the same chapter with many words, and then passed over to the commendation of the dead, as is clear in the text.

The third passage is 1 Kings (1 Samuel) 31:13, in the last chapter, where we read that the inhabitants of Jabes Galaad, having heard about the death of Saul, fasted for seven days. And in 2 Kings (2 Samuel) 1:12, David wept and fasted for Saul and Jonathan after they were killed, and

Ch. III: Purgatory proven from the Old Testament

he did the same for Abner in 2 Kings 3:35. Although these seem to be done as a sign of sorrow and sadness, nevertheless, it is believable that it was especially done to help the souls of the dead, as Bede explains at the end of his commentary on the first book of Kings, and thus we gather two points from it. 1) It would be unreasonable to fast for seven days as a sign of sorrow; 2) from what David did in 2 Kings 12:20 when he fasted and prayed for his infant son, while he was sick, but later, when he heard it died, he no longer fasted, from which fact he showed that he customarily fasted in order to ask something of God; therefore, he did not fast after the death of the child because he knew it could not be returned to life and did not need prayers. This is also seen in the solicitude of the patriarchs, who desired to be buried in the promised land (Gen. 47:30 & 50:5), surely that they might be partakers of the prayers and sacrifices which were offered there.

The fourth passage is Psalm 37: "Rebuke me not, O Lord, in your indignation; nor chastise me in your wrath." Even if these words can be explained differently, nevertheless, St. Augustine so explains them that to be rebuked by God in indignation, means in eternal damnation; to be chastised in wrath, to be severely punished after this life, for correction and emendation. Wherefore, he adds: "In this life, cleanse me, render me such that I shall not need the corrective fire." In the same way Bede, Haymo, Dionysius the Carthusian, and others explain this passage.

The fifth passage is Psalm 65(66):11, "We passed through fire and water, and you led us into rest." This passage can also have many senses, nevertheless, Origen (hom. 25 in num.) and St. Ambrose (in Ps. 36 and ser. 3 in Ps. 118) explain by water, Baptism, but by fire, Purgatory:

"The latter," he says, "through water, the former, through fire, through water to wash away sins, through fire that they might be burned."

The sixth passage is Isaiah 4:4, "The Lord will cleanse the filth of the sons and daughters of Sion, and will cleanse the blood from their midst by the spirit of judgment, and the spirit of burning." St. Augustine explains this passage to be about Purgatory in *City of God*, book 20 cap. 25.

The seventh passage is Isaiah 9:18, "Impiety burns as a fire and devours thorns." St. Basil says on this passage that through confession sin withers away, so that it can be taken away by a purgatorial fire after this life, and he proves it from this passage.

The eighth passage is of Micah 7:8, "O my enemy, do not rejoice over me; for if I am fallen, I shall arise; when I sit in darkness, I will bear the wrath of the Lord, until he judges my cause. He will lead me forth into light; I will see his justice." This passage is usually adduced in favor of Purgatory, as St. Jerome teaches in the final chapter of Isaiah, and the *Glossa Ordinaria* explains it: I will bear the Lord's anger here or in Purgatory.

The ninth passage is Zachariah 9:12, "You also, by the blood of your covenant, have led those bound out of the pit wherein there is no water."[3] Even if they normally adduce

---

[3] Translator's note: this is the translation from the text Bellarmine cites, "Tu autem in sanguine Testamenti tui eduxisti vinctos tuos de lacu, in quo non est aqua." The text of the Clementine Vulgate, revised and promulgated after this book was written, has: "Tu quoque in sanguine testamenti tui emisisti vinctos tuos de lacu in quo non est aqua," or as the revised Douay-Rheims has it: "Thou also, by the blood of thy testament, hath sent forth thy prisoners out of the pit wherein there is no water."

this passage for the liberation of the fathers from limbo, nevertheless it agrees better with the liberation of souls from Purgatory, whom Christ lead out when he descended after his death. Firstly, because the souls in purgatory are more rightly said to be bound; secondly, because in Purgatory there is no water of consolation, as there is in limbo, as is clear from Luke 16:25, in regard to Lazarus: "Here he is consoled." Wherefore, Augustine contends that Christ, when he descended to hell, not only visited the fathers, but even those who were tortured in hell, that is, in Purgatory, and freed many of them from there (epist. 99 ad Evodium, and in Genes. lib. 42 cap. 33).

The tenth passage is Malachi 3:3, "He will sit as a burning fire, and will cleanse the sons of Levi, and will purify them, etc." Origen (hom. 6 in Exod.), St. Ambrose (in Ps. 36), St. Augustine (*de Civitate Dei*, l. 20, cap. 25) and St. Jerome, explain this passage as about purgatorial punishment, and although those purgatorial punishments are not those which we are now arguing about (since they will cleanse the living, whereas we argue on the punishment of the dead), nevertheless purgatory is rightly inferred from there. For on that account, at the time when the final tribulation runs its course, afterwards the fire will also descend and quickly purge all the remnants of sins in just men, since, as Irenaeus also notes at the end of book 5, then the Church on earth will immediately be taken to her spouse, and there will no longer be a time of further purgation, as there is now after death and before the Judgment.

CHAPTER IV
Purgatory is Proven from the New Testament

HE *first passage* is Matthew 12:32, where the Lord says there is a certain sin which is not remitted, neither in this age nor in the coming age. From here, the holy Fathers gather that certain sins are remitted in the future age through the prayers and offerings of the Church (St. Augustine, *de Civitate Dei*, lib. 21 c. 24 et *in Julianum*, lib. 6, c. 5; St. Gregory, *Dialog*. lib. 4, c. 39; St. Bede in Mar. c. 3; St. Bernard, hom. 66 *in Cant.*, who was content with this testimony alone against the heresy which denies Purgatory. Likewise Peter the Cluniac, *in epist. contra Petrobrusianos*; Rabanus, *de Instit. Cleric.* lib. 2 c. 44, and all the Glosses, such as the ordinary and interlinear, etc.).

But there are several objections to this. *Firstly*, Peter Martyr argues that Christ spoke by way of exaggeration.

I respond: In this way we can also abolish hell, and say it was an exaggeration when the Lord said, "Go into the eternal fire." Besides, an exaggeration ought not to be inept, such as when a partition is made and nothing corresponds to one part.

Secondly, some say it is said to be a threat.

I respond: We answer just as we did the first objection.

Thirdly, others object that Christ compares the sin against the Holy Spirit with the most serious mortal sins, with blasphemy against the Father and the Son; therefore, if he meant to say some sins can be remitted in another age, he particularly understood this about those to which he compared the sin against the Holy Spirit at that time;

Ch. IV: Purgatory is proven from the New Testament 27

but this is false, because only venial sins are forgiven us in another age, etc.

I respond: Christ spoke of the perfect remission which embraces the remission of guilt and punishment, which is how the most serious sins are remitted in another age, because there their remission is completed.

Fourthly, they say that Christ would seem to mean that more serious sins are remitted in the coming age, but in this one only lighter ones, if he meant that some are remitted there, otherwise he would not have said, "Neither in this age, nor in the coming age"; on the contrary he would have said it will not be forgiven either in the coming age or in this one, that the discourse might crescendo.

I respond: The discourse builds to a climax because in the coming age there is a greater space to wash away sins than here, and besides, this age is put first because the remission of sins begins here, but it is completed there.

Fifthly, Calvin objects that the Lord spoke about the remission of guilt, consequently, this passage is wrongly alleged for the remission of the punishment of purgatory.

I respond: In purgatory at least venial sins are remitted; besides, it is false that Christ spoke only about guilt. For this is the sense: sin against the Holy Spirit is not remitted in this age nor in the coming age, neither in regard to guilt, nor in regard to punishment, although other sins are either remitted in this age in regard to guilt, and in another in regard to punishment, such as mortal sins; or remitted both in this life and the next in regard to guilt, and in regard to punishment, such as venial sins.

Sixthly, Calvin says that by "in this age and in the coming one," he meant to say, in this judgment and in the final judgment it will not be remitted, and so no mention is made of purgatory. On the other hand, who are they, for whom the sin is not remitted here, and for whom it will be remitted in the judgment? Is it not those who either need purgation of venial sins or, who only owe a debt of punishment? For whoever leaves this life in unrighteousness, certainly will not be absolved in the judgment.

Seventhly, Peter Martyr objects: since in good Logic an affirmation does not follow from a negation, therefore one may not infer that because the sin against the Holy Spirit is not remitted in the coming age, therefore certain other sins can be remitted there. In the same way, it does not rightly follow that King Philip is not king of the Venetians, therefore someone else is king of the Venetians. And Ochinus confirms it; for Christ could say: This sin is not remitted in this age, nor in hell, yet we would not gather that certain sins are remitted in hell.

I respond: What we infer from the Lord's words may not follow according to the rules of the logicians, nevertheless it follows according to the rule of prudence, because otherwise we would make the Lord the ineptest of speakers. If nothing is remitted in the coming age, then he said ineptly: This sin will not be remitted in this age nor in the coming one. Just as one would speak ineptly if he were to say: King Philip does not absolve you either in the court of Spain or of France. But he would not speak ineptly if he were to say: Either in the court of Spain, or in that of Brabant.[4] Hence, in John 18:36, when Christ said: "My kingdom is not of this world," Pilate inferred: "So you are

---

[4] Translator's note: The Brabant Bellarmine is referring to is a province of Flanders (Belgium), and thus under the authority of Spain at the time of the book's writing.

Ch. IV: Purgatory is proven from the New Testament   29

a king?" Christ did not respond that an affirmative does not rightly follow from a negative, rather he approved it. Nor does the similitude brought by Ochinus avail since Christ could not say: Neither in this age nor in hell, unless he meant to speak ineptly, firstly because an age is a time but hell a place; hence they are not opposed like the present age and the future age, then besides, because it is certain that no remission of sins takes place in hell.

Eighthly, they object that, "Neither in this age nor in the coming one," mean the same thing, which is never, or forever (*in aeternum*), as Mark shows, who in 3:29 says, "He will never (*non in aeternum*) have remission." And as Peter says in John 13:8, "You will never (*non in aeternum*) wash my feet."

I respond: One ought not to explain Matthew by Mark but rather Mark by Matthew, since Matthew uses many more words and it is certain he wrote more copiously, whereas Mark made something like a compendium from the Gospel of Matthew. Nor did Mark use the expression "*in aeternum*" in the same sense as Peter in John's Gospel. For Peter would have spoken ineptly if he were to say: You will not wash my feet, neither in this age nor in the next, although feet are not going to be washed in the coming age. But the Lord did not speak ineptly in Matthew when he said: "It will not be remitted, neither in this age nor in the coming age." Consequently, Peter in John's gospel takes the term: "*In aeternum*" improperly for the time of this life only, but Mark properly for the whole space of this age and the coming age. Besides, Christ either spoke as Matthew has it, or as Mark has it, or in each mode; if first or third, I hold it was intended; if the second, although this is not probable, then Matthew, led by the Holy Spirit, explained the words of Christ, and unless he explained ineptly, he indicated some sins are forgiven in another age.

Ninth, they say it is a Hebrew expression.

I respond: This is false. It is indeed a Hebrew expression when Peter says, "*In aeternum*", for the Jews say everywhere: לעולם [lehholam] even about temporal things; "But neither in this age, nor in the next," is not a proper Hebrew expression. Nor did Mark use a Hebrew expression, rather, he spoke properly.

CHAPTER V
1 Corinthians 3:15

THE second passage is 1 Corinthians 3:15, where the Apostle says, "He himself will be saved, yet so as by fire." In the first place, note that the passage of the Apostle is one of the most difficult and useful of the whole Scripture, for Catholics establish two ecclesiastical dogmas from it: purgatory and venial sins, against the heretics and the supporters of heretics, such as Erasmus was at first, who in his annotation on this passage tried to show that neither purgatory nor venial sins could be established from it.

Augustine attests to the fact that it is a very difficult passage in his book on *Faith and Works* (c. 15) where he says: "We must attend diligently, how that teaching of the Apostle Paul must be received which is clearly difficult to understand, where he says: "If anyone builds upon this foundation, gold, silver, etc. ... In these places we must pay heed to what Peter says, that certain things in the Scriptures are very difficult, and men ought not pervert them to their own destruction. ... I affirm, that I prefer to listen to those who are more intelligent and more learned." He repeats the same thing in q. 1 *ad Dulcitium*.

Therefore, that we might diligently explain this passage, we will first explain the metaphor which the Apostle used; then we will propose and answer difficulties which occur in regard to this passage. As to the *first*, then, these are the words of the Apostle: "According to the grace of God, which was given to me, as a wise architect I placed a foundation, and another builds upon it, but let every man look to how he builds upon it; for no man can place another foundation apart from that which had been laid, which is Christ Jesus. So, if anyone builds upon this foundation, gold, silver, precious stones, wood, grass, straw, the work of every man will be made manifest. For the day of the Lord will declare it, because it will be revealed in fire, and fire will prove every man's work, of what sort it is. If anyone's work will remain, which had been built upon it, he will receive his reward; if anyone's work will burn, he will suffer detriment, but he himself will be saved, yet so as by fire."

The Apostle uses in this teaching a similitude of two architects, one of whom, upon a solid stone foundation, built a house out of precious materials which do not fear fire, such as are gold, and silver, and precious stones such as Jasper, Porphyry, Parian marble. For from gold and silver plates and pillars are made, as we read about the temple of Solomon. From Parian marble and porphyry even whole walls can be erected. Another architect, upon a similar foundation, namely a solid stone one, erected a house in the manner of poor country-folk out of stakes and boards, and covered it with grass and straw.

Now that we have posited this similitude, let us imagine that fire is applied to each house, and we will see that the first one is completely unharmed, and if the architect is by chance inside, he similarly will suffer nothing. But we will see the second house will immediately catch fire and the whole shall be burnt up in a short time, and if the Architect is inside and wishes to get out safe, we will see that he cannot go out, except through the fire. In such a passage he indeed will not die, but still his beard and hair will not escape unharmed, unless perhaps the miracle of the three children, who were not burned in the furnace in Babylon, is repeated. This is the similitude which St. Paul uses when he says, "He himself will be saved, yet so as by fire."

In regard to the *second*, there are five difficulties. First, who is meant by the builders; second, what is meant by gold, silver, precious stones, wood, grass and straw; third, what is meant by the day of the Lord; fourth, what is meant by the fire, which on the day of the Lord will prove every man's work; fifth, what is meant by the fire, about which it is said: "he himself will be saved, yet so as by fire." After we have explained these, the teaching will be clear.

The first difficulty is, who are the architects that build? St. Augustine, in his book *on Faith and Works*, ch. 16, as well as in *Enchririd.*, cap. 68, and elsewhere, thinks that all Christians are called architects by the Apostle, and all build upon the foundation of faith either good works or bad works. It seems to me that Chrysostom, Theodoret, Theophylactus, and Oecumenius teach the same thing on this passage.

Many others teach that here the Apostle only calls doctors and preachers of the Gospel architects. So think Ambrose, and Sedulius on this passage. Jerome insinuates the same thing *in Iovinianum*, lib. 2. St. Anselm and St. Thomas receive the same thing on this passage, even though they do not reject the prior opinion. Many more recent authors teach the same thing on this passage, such as Dennis the Carthusian, Lyranus and Cajetan.

Each exposition is good and from each exposition the assertion of purgatory and venial sins can be deduced, nevertheless the second is more literal, which is manifestly clear from the preceding and following words of the chapter. For he had said earlier: "I planted, Apollo watered." Then, in the same sense he immediately added: "I as a wise architect placed a foundation, but another builds upon it." And likewise: "He who plants and he who waters are equal; each shall receive his own reward according to his labor, for we are helpers of God, you are the field of God, you are the building of God." There he very clearly compares himself and other preachers of the Gospel to farmers and architects, but the people who are taught he compares to fields and buildings. Likewise, in the following words he again speaks about teachers when he says: "If anyone seems wise among you, let him be a fool so that he might become wise." And again, "Let no man boast of men, for all are yours, whether Paul, or Apollo or Cephas", *i.e.* do not boast in your teachers and preachers, and say: "I am of Paul, but I of Apollo." For all are one and they all labor for you. Therefore, just as he had said that he planted and Apollo watered, so now he says, I placed the foundation by preaching the faith of Christ, but others build upon it by teaching those things which pertain to life and morals, and even explaining more fully the mysteries of faith. And in this first question Calvin, Peter Martyr, and Ochinus agree with us.

The second difficulty is a little more serious, and there are six opinions. Certain men understand by the term "foundation" the true faith, but unformed. By the terms gold, silver, and precious stones, good works. By wood, grass, and straw, mortal sins; Chrysostom so thinks on this passage, whom Theophylactus follows.

But this cannot be defended. 1) Because, as St. Gregory says (lib. 4 *Dialog.* c. 39), mortal sins are better compared with iron and lead. 2) Because it would follow that the heresy of Origen is true that all men are saved, since the Apostle says, "He will be saved as if by fire."

The Greeks respond that he will be saved, *i.e.*, never be altogether consumed, yet so as by fire, since he will burn forever. This answer is especially hard and forced; then also it is against every manner of speaking in the Scriptures. For in Scripture, the word salvation is never received in a bad sense, but always in a good, as the Latin theologians showed at the Council of Florence before the first session. Besides, the word "by" (*per*) means the passage, not the lodging. The Apostle does not say he will be saved, yet as if *in* the fire, but "he will be saved, yet as if *by* fire," *i.e.*, according to the similitude, he evades death by passing through fire. Finally, from the common consent of the Doctors. For all others in the greatest consensus, both Greeks and Latins, would have it that this passage be understood of venial sins, whose opinions we will present in the fifth difficulty. Furthermore, let no one think from this discussion that Chrysostom denied purgatory or venial sins. For he frequently teaches purgatory, and especially in homil. 3, on epist. to Philipp., and hom. 69 to the people of Antioch. Likewise, he concedes venial sins (hom. 24 in Matth.), but on this passage he explained it otherwise to refute the heresy of Origen, which taught that the penalties of hell are not eternal, as is clear in the homily.

The second opinion is that by the term foundation Christ is to be understood, or the preaching of the faith, while "silver, gold and precious stones" refer to Catholic expositions; "wood, grass, and straw" are understood to be heretical doctrines, as the commentary of Ambrose seems to teach, and also Jerome explaining Isaiah 5:8, "Woe unto you that join house to house." Also inclining to this opinion are Calvin, Peter Martyr and Ochinus, who teach that by wood, grass, and straw we should understand human traditions and inventions opposed to the word of God.

This opinion is even less defensible than the previous one. *Firstly*, because heretics are not saved by the fire of purgatory, but are condemned to eternal fire. *Secondly*, because heretics do not build upon the foundation, which is Christ, except in name only. For every heresy speaks wonderfully about Christ, yet does not preach the true Christ, but another which it invents for itself. Nor are these opinions that we refute those of Ambrose and Jerome, since the commentary of Ambrose understands by "wood, grass, and straw" heresies and false doctrines advanced out of imprudence and without pertinacity, for he says teachers of this kind will be saved by the purgatorial fire. On the other hand, Jerome clearly speaks about heretics, but according to the mind of others, not his own, since when he posits his own exposition, he adds: "But certain others understand this to be about heretics, etc."

The third opinion understands living faith for the word "foundation". For gold, silver and precious stones it understands works of supererogation; by wood, grass, and straw it understands the omission of counsel and a certain carnal attachment to the goods of this world which are indeed licit, but which bring sorrow when they are lost. So Augustine thinks in his book *on Faith and Works*, c. 16. Such an opinion is true, but it does not fit this passage, unless we are to understand by that carnal attachment at least venial sins, for neutral works are not spoken of in particular. Therefore, that carnal love is either good or bad:

if good, why will it burn after the fashion of straw? If bad, then at least it has been mixed with venial sin.

The fourth opinion is that of those who explain by gold, silver, etc. to be good works, but by straw, grass, etc., venial sins. This is what St. Gregory thinks (*Dialogue*, book 4, c. 39) and others, which is good, but another opinion is better.

The fifth opinion is that of those who understand gold, silver, etc. to be good students of the word, but straw, bad students. The students are the workmanship of the teacher, and indeed the teacher will be saved; but some of the students will, and some will not. So think Theodoret and Oecumenius, but Chrysostom rightly refutes this; for "loss" is attributed to the architect, and he himself is said to have built with straw, therefore the guilt and punishment is not that of the hearers alone.

The sixth opinion, which we put ahead of all the rest, understands Christ by the foundation, announced by the first preachers, such as were the Apostles, who conveyed the faith and Gospel of Christ to those peoples who had never heard of Christ. Hence, St. Paul says: "I planted" and "I, as a wise architect, placed the foundation." Hence, those also who first preached the faith in some region are said to be the apostles of that region. Then, by gold, silver, and precious stones, is meant the useful and salutary doctrine of other preachers, who teach those who have already received the faith, and who teach not only by word, but also by example, so that they truly build up their students and further them in religion and piety. But by wood, grass and straw, is understood the teaching, not heretical or bad, yet curious, useless, and vain, of those preachers who preach to the Catholic people in a Catholic manner, but without that fruit and usefulness which God requires. As a result, the former preach with great merit, but these preach not only without great merit, but even not without venial sins.

Three things most especially prove this exposition. 1) Because, as we will show, by the term "builders", only teachers are understood, therefore by the term "their work", their doctrine ought to be understood.

2) This similitude thus explained is very appropriate for the doctors of Corinth. For they were more favorably given to eloquence and philosophy which, although it is permitted to make use of them, nevertheless sometimes impede the fruit of preaching, and St. Paul rebuked the Corinthians because of both things in this epistle.

3) Because this whole chapter is best explained if St. Paul posits three similitudes: a) of farmers planting and watering, which only embraces good teachers; b) on builders building upon a good foundation, which embraces both good and bad teachers; c) on the corruptors of the temple, in which he meant only the bad to be included, and not bad by a certain measure, but completely bad, such as heretics teaching error for truth and vices for virtues, about whom he does not say they shall be saved, as if by fire, but that God will destroy them.

The third difficulty is in regard to the "day of the Lord". Some understand by the word "day" the present life, or the time of tribulation in which the good are often picked out from the bad, such as St. Augustine (*de fide et operibus*, cap. 16), and St. Gregory (*Dialogue* lib. 4, ch. 39).

This opinion does not seem to be according to the mind of St. Paul. 1) In Greek "day" is with the article, ἡ γαρ ἡμέρα, from which it appears that a certain and defined day is meant, just as in 2 Tim. 4:8, "Which the Lord will render to me on that day," and in 2 Tim. 1:12 "I am certain that he is able to keep what has been entrusted to me until that day." And below, "May the Lord grant that he may find mercy on that day."

2) The present time is not called the day of the Lord in the Scriptures, but rather our day, just as, on the other hand, the time of the next life is called the day of the Lord, not ours, such as in Luke 19:42, "And indeed on this your day, the things which are to your peace;" Luke 22:53, "This is your hour;" Galatians 6:10, "While we have time, let us do good;" Psalm 74 (75):2, "When I appoint a time, then I will judge with justice;" Zephaniah 1:14, "The great day of the Lord is near;" and Joel 2:1, "The day of the Lord will come, the day of darkness and gloom."

3) The quality of everyone's work shall not be declared in the time of the present life. For tribulations are common to good and evil, just and unjust.

4) All doctors understand this day to be the day of judgment; for although Augustine and Gregory taught that the day could be referred to this life, nevertheless, they teach in the same places that it can also be understood of the time to come after this life. In fact, since the day of judgment is two-fold, one day of the particular judgment and another day of the universal judgment, then, as Cajetan and others say, the Apostle speaks of the day of the particular judgment. a) Because after this day of which the Apostle speaks, some are going to be purged by fire; but that cannot be after the day of the last judgment. b) Because if this day, which the Apostle speaks about, were the day of the final judgment, it would follow that none of the saints could enter into heaven before the day of

judgment, which is an error condemned at the Council of Florence, in the last session. The consequent is proved; for on this day all buildings are to be examined, and after the examination some are going to be immediately crowned while others are punished; besides, since nothing polluted shall enter into the kingdom of heaven, if a purgation of venial sins does not take place except on the day of the last judgment, all who leave this life with venial sins should await that day before they can enter into heaven.

c) Because the Greek text does not have "it will be revealed," but it is revealed: "Ὅτι ἐν περὶ ἀποκαλύπτεται," because it is revealed in the fire. But the day of the last judgment is not revealed, thus, he speaks of the day of the particular judgment, which is revealed every day, now to one, now to another. Nevertheless, all the older authors seem to understand by that day the day of the last judgment, such as Theodoret, Theophylactus, Anselm and others, whose opinion seems quite true to me, although neither opinion opposes purgatory.

Firstly, because everywhere in the Scriptures, the day of the Lord means the day of the last judgment.

Secondly, because it is said "on that day," by which one certain day is designated, on which the works of all men shall be proved at once; but the day of the particular judgment is not one, but manifold, nor are the works of all men proved on it.

Thirdly, because the Apostle says: "The day of the Lord will declare," in other words, then all things will be manifested to everyone, as he says in the following chapter: "Until the Lord shall come, who will bring to light what is hidden in darkness, and manifest the counsels of hearts," but that will not take place except in the last judgment.

Fourthly, because it follows in verse 13: "Because it will be revealed in fire." For the day of judgment is said to be revealed in fire, since the conflagration of the whole world will be the last sign and it will be made known to all, which is why the day of judgment is almost always described by fire, such as in Psalm 96 (97):3, "Fire will precede him;" Joel 2:3, "The consuming fire before his face;" 2 Thessalonians 1:7, "In the revelation of our Lord Jesus Christ from heaven with his powerful angels in the flame of fire;" 2 Peter 3:12, "The elements will melt in the flame of fire." And if it does not please one to accept here a material flame for the fire, but rather the judgment of God itself, as others explain, still only the last judgment can be understood by "this day". For then, the sense is that it is revealed in fire, *i.e.* because that day will be notorious on account of the great and bitter judgment which will be exercised on it; but the day of the particular judgment is not notorious on account of judgment, but rather on account of death, since the particular judgment is known to few. The arguments to the contrary do not move me.

To the first, I say, after the last judgment there will be no purgatory, and therefore those words: "He will be saved, yet as if by fire," do not mean he will be saved provided he first passes through fire, but he will be saved provided earlier he passed through fire; or, he will be saved, just as those who pass through fire.

To the second, I say if one were to concluded this, it would follow that even if there were no purgatory, no one is beatified or condemned before the day of judgment; for Scripture everywhere attributes the distribution of rewards and punishments to the last judgment; nay more, even an examination of the works, and the sentence of the judge, as is clear from Matthew 25:41 and elsewhere. Therefore, just as sentence is pronounced upon the death of anyone, and then some men begin to be punished, and some rewarded, and nevertheless these same things are said to happen in the last judgment because then they will occur in the presence of the whole world, and with the greatest honor for the just but the greatest ignominy for the impious, so also the examination can take place at the death of everyone privately, and later again publicly in the final judgment.

To the third I say, for the one word which we have in the present tense in Greek we have three in the future, namely: φανερὸν γερήσεται, ἡμέρα δηλώσει. ... πῦρ δοκιμάσει; and it is also very believable that this one word ἀποκαλύπτεται in the more correct texts was in the future tense, ἀποκαλύψεται, seeing that our translator rendered it "it will be revealed" (*revelabitur*). Add, that frequently the present tense is not used to mean an action of a certain time, but a custom, opinion, profession, or something similar, *e.g.* "I do not know man," as the Blessed Virgin says (Luke 1), and what the Sadducees said: "The dead do not rise," or, what the Carthusians say: "We do not eat meat." In this difficulty we dissent from Calvin and Peter Martyr, since they understand Paul to be speaking of the particular judgment, but this does nothing for the question on purgatory.

The fourth difficulty is what is the fire, which will prove every man's work on the day of the Lord? Some understand the tribulations of this life, such as St. Augustine and St. Gregory (*ll. cc.*), but we already rejected this. Others understand eternal fire, but that cannot be since that fire will not examine the building made of gold and silver, nor even the building made of wood and grass, as is clear. Others seem to understand the fire as the conflagration of the world, which precedes the general judgment. That also cannot be, because that fire does not burn anyone except the enemies of God, as we read in Psalm 96 (97):3, "The fire precedes him, and will burn his enemies all around." But this fire, of which the Apostle speaks, touches everyone, even those who built upon the foundation with gold and silver. Besides, that fire cannot prove works, since it is a material fire and works will not exist anywhere but the mind, because they have passed away.

Others understand it as referring to the punishments of purgatory, but neither can this rightly be said. *a*) Because the fire of purgatory does not prove the works of those who build with gold and silver, whereas the fire which we are talking about, "will prove the quality of every man's work." *b*) The Apostle clearly distinguishes between works and workers, and he says about that fire that it burns works, not workers, for he says: "If anyone's work remains," and "if anyone's work burns." But the fire of purgatory, which is a true and real fire, cannot burn works because they are transitory actions and they have already passed.

Next, it would follow that all men, even the holiest, pass through the fire of purgatory and are saved through the fire, for all pass through this fire of which we speak. Yet that all pass through the fire of purgatory and are saved by the fire is clearly false, since in this passage the Apostle clearly says only those who built with wood and grass are going to be saved as if by fire. Moreover, the Church has always understood that the holy martyrs as well as infants dying after baptism are immediately received into heaven without any passage through fire, as the Council of Florence teaches (final session). The Holy Fathers, St. Jerome (*in Jovin.* lib. 2) and St. Augustine (in Psalm 37/38) also teach this. St. Augustine says: "If they built with gold, silver, or precious stones, they will be safe from both fires, not only from the eternal one, which is going to torture the impious forever, but also from that which will correct those who are saved by fire."

Consequently, it remains for us to say that here the Apostle speaks of the fire of the severe and just judgment of God, which is not a cleansing or afflicting fire, but an examining and proving one. St. Ambrose explains it this way in Sermon 20 on Psalm 118 (119), on the verse *Vide humilitatem meam*, "The furnace will prove all of us, therefore, because we are going to be examined, so let us act that we may be worthy to be proved by the divine judgment; let us possess the humility here depicted, so that when each and every one of us shall come to the judgment of God, to those fires that we are going to pass through, he may say, 'see my humility,' etc." Sedulius speaks likewise on this verse: "He wished to compare the examination of judgment to a fire, according to the custom of the Scriptures." Dennis the Carthusian, Lyranus, Cajetan and others give the same exposition on this passage.

That this position is the truest is proven by the following:

a) Because it cannot be understood otherwise how the fire proves those that built with gold and silver.

b) Because this exposition best fits the words of the Apostle, when he says: "Fire will prove the quality of every man's work. If anyone's work will remain, he will receive his reward; if anyone's work will burn, he will suffer detriment." For, although their works have passed before the eyes of men, and cannot be examined by a material fire, nevertheless, they have not passed before the eyes of God, but, as it is said in Ecclesiastes 12:14, "All the things that are done, God will bring to judgment," and he will examine them, and if someone's "work will remain," that is, if the work can withstand the judgment of God, as gold withstands fire, he will receive his reward and be proved and crowned by God. If anyone's work burns, *i.e.* if someone's work does not withstand the judgment of God, as grass and straw do not withstand fire, he will suffer detriment, and be reproved and rejected.

c) Because the judgment of God is most rightly called a fire, seeing that it is the purest, quickest, most efficacious, and most penetrating. This is why we read in Daniel: "A fiery river will proceed from his mouth" (Daniel 7:10).[5] And because God is all justice, all judgment, therefore He also is called a fire in the Scriptures. "He is like a refining fire" (Malachi 3:2). "For our God is a consuming fire" (Hebrews 12:29). And in this we do not dissent from Calvin and Peter Martyr.

The fifth and final difficulty is, what is understood by fire, when he says: "And he will be saved, yet as if by fire."

---

[5] Translator's note: The Vulgate Bellarmine uses reads: "*Fluvius igneus egredietur de ore ejus.*" However, the revised edition subsequent to Bellarmine's writing reads: "*Fluvius igneus rapidusque egrediebatur a facie ejus*," or, "A swift fiery stream proceeded from his face."

Some understand the tribulations of this life. But this cannot be said congruently, because then also those who build with gold and silver would be saved, as if by fire. Accordingly, St. Augustine and St. Gregory, who are the authors of this opinion, although they do not relinquish it, also advance another opinion which we will relate below. Some understand the eternal fire, such as Chrysostom and Theophylactus, but we have already refuted this. Others the fire of the conflagration of the world. That also cannot be said on account of the reasons we posited previously; besides, it would follow that those who have venial sins could not attain to beatitude before the day of judgment, seeing that nothing impure can enter into heaven.

Calvin and Peter Martyr, as well as Ochinus and Luther (arctic. 37) understand by this fire the judgment of God, which sanctions true doctrine and confutes false, just as fire finishes gold and consumes grass. Moreover, they say this judgment takes place when someone is converted, and especially in the hour of death, for then many are enlightened and so understand that they were deceived, and throw away their doctrine, and are also confounded and blush, and so will be saved by fire. Peter Martyr adds that he does not doubt that St. Bernard, St. Francis, St. Dominic and other fathers were saved in this way, since without a doubt, being enlightened by God at the point of death, they understood and condemned their errors on monasticism, on the Mass, etc.

Sed contra: 1) Since that judgment would only happen at the time of death, it either happens while the man is still alive, or it could also take place after death. If it could also happen after death, therefore, after death there is some remission and purgation of sins, at least through that

Ch. V: 1 Corinthians 3:15

shame and contrition, which they will in no way admit, for this would be a certain type of Purgatory. But if this judgment would only happen during death itself, how, I ask, would it happen with those men who built upon the foundation with wood, grass, and straw but died so suddenly that they had no time for repentance? They are not saved as if by fire, who do not experience this fire of judgment and refutation of their errors, nor can they be condemned to hell because they had Christ as a foundation, and Paul declares about all such men that they would be saved. Indeed, it is not possible for them to be saved unless Purgatory is admitted, for since they died in sin with their straw and grass, they cannot be saved except by fire.

2) That fire, which Paul is speaking about, will properly and truly inflict penalties apart from the loss of their works, and the shame which thence arises, therefore that judgment refuting their errors is not the fire which is treated on here. The preceding is proven firstly from that phrase: "he will suffer detriment," which in Greek is ζημιωθήσεται, he will be punished, or he will pay penalties. Few words are more frequent in Greek than ζημοῦσθαι θανάτῳ, that is to be punished with death. Likewise, from that: "He will be saved, as if by fire." The similitude of one passing through fire means punishment and sorrow, for he that passes through fire without any harm, would not be said to pass through fire, as through fire, but as if through flowers, as we read about St. Tiburtius.

3) The Apostle opposes this passage through fire to the reward. As he had said: "If his work will remain, he will receive his reward," so now he says, "if his work burns, he

will suffer detriment and he will be saved as if by fire." But that reward means something apart from the good work, and apart from the joy which the good work produces of itself, since he would not say he will receive the reward if the reward were nothing else than what he had from the act of building with gold, etc., itself. Consequently, the detriment and the passage through fire of the man who built with straw, is likewise some punishment apart from the loss of the works, and apart from the shame it produces of itself.

4) Because that judgment refuting errors does not bring detriment, but profit, for it is a certain enlightenment of the mind, as they say, and a knowledge of the truth. And as a man that has brass thinking that it is gold does not think it is a loss, if someone would take away that brass and would give him true gold, so also one that had errors in his mind and learns the truth by divine illustration does not suffer detriment, but acquires profit. But Paul says: "He will suffer a detriment," therefore, etc.

5) It would follow that everyone that is saved is saved as if by fire, which is contrary to the distinction of the Apostle, for even if here Paul only treats on sins which are committed in teaching, nevertheless, the reasoning for all other sins is the same. For as God will judge doctrine, so also all works. But according to Calvin, and all Lutherans, all of our works, no matter how just they seem in the eyes of men, are still sins in the sight of God, nor can they bear divine judgment, rather, they will be clearly convicted in the way false doctrine is. This is why if the fire, about which Paul is speaking, is the judgment of God, all will be saved as if by fire. Nor does the response avail that the works of the just are not going to be convicted, because

they are covered over through non-imputation, but the works of the impious who are not justified by faith are going to be convicted; for when Paul says, "He will be saved, as if by fire," he speaks about the just who built with straw, yet having retained the foundation, namely, true faith in Christ.

Now, what Peter Martyr says about Sts. Bernard, Dominic, and Francis, is a most impudent lie, since even to their last breath they commended to their followers perseverance in religious life and obedience to the Roman Church. In chapter 14 of his life, St. Bonaventure writes about St. Francis: "With the hour of his passage nearing, he caused all the brethren present in that place to be called to himself, and soothing them with consoling words on account of his death, he exhorted them with paternal affection to divine love, and he spoke at length on patience, poverty, and the faith of the holy Roman Church which must be kept, and above all, he added, 'Remain strong, all ye my sons, in the fear of the Lord, and remain in him always, and since temptation will come and tribulation approaches, happy are they who will persevere in what they have begun. Now I hasten to God, to whose grace I commend you.'" This must surely be the recantation which the Pseudomartyr Peter dreams up!

Now it is the common teaching of Theologians that by the term "fire" in this passage some purgatorial and temporal punishment is understood, to which those who are found in the particular judgment to have built with wood, grass or straw are assigned after death. This exposition, apart from the fact that it best agrees with the text, is sufficiently proven from the common consensus of the Fathers. All Latins teach this. St. Cyprian, in his epistle to Antoninus (book 4, ep. 2) says: "It is one thing to stand for pardon, another to attain to glory; it is one thing to be thrown into prison and not get out until one pays the last penny, but another to immediately receive the reward for faith and virtue; it is one thing, having been crucified by long suffering, to be corrected for sins, and to be purged at length by fire, and another to be cleansed of all sins by martyrdom." Here, Cyprian does not clearly call to mind this passage of St. Paul, but nevertheless, since nowhere else in Scripture is mention made of fire in a passage which is clearly about Purgatory, there is no doubt that St. Cyprian alluded to this passage.

St. Ambrose, commenting on this passage, says: "But when Paul says 'yet as if by fire', he shows indeed that he is going to be saved, but he will suffer the punishments of the fire, so that having been purged by the fire he will be saved, not tormented in the eternal fire forever like the faithless." He says the same thing in Serm. 20 in Psalm 118.

St. Jerome, while explaining "You have become just as a firebrand taken from the fire" explaining Amos chapter 4 says, "Like what we read in the Apostle, he will be saved as if by fire, therefore whoever is saved by fire, is taken out just as a firebrand from the fire." He taught the same thing while commenting on the last book of Isaiah, and in book 2 *in Jovinianum*, just past the middle.

St. Augustine, in Psalm 37 (38) says: "In this life may you cleanse me, and render me such that a cleansing fire is no longer needed." And below, while explaining the passage of the Apostle, he says, "It is related that he will be saved as if by fire, and because it is said, 'he will be saved', that fire is disregarded. For all that, though he is saved by the fire, yet that fire will be more grievous than anything a

Ch. V: 1 Corinthians 3:15 51

man can suffer in this life." St. Gregory the Great, in book 4 of the *Dialogue* (c. 39), while explaining this passage of 1 Cor. 3:15, says: "Although this passage could be understood of the fire of tribulation applied to us in this life, nevertheless, if someone were to take it as referring to the fire of future purgation, it must be carefully considered, because by that fire he is said be saved, not who builds upon this [foundation] with iron, bronze, or lead, that is, greater sins, and on that account harder, and hence impossible to be loosed, but wood, grass and straw, *i.e.* minute sins, and the very lightest, which the fire easily consumes."

Alcuin (lib. 3 *de Trinitate*), Rupert (in. 3.c. *Gen.*, explaining that which is said there on the flaming and revolving sword), Peter Lombard (4 d. 21) and with him St. Bonaventure and other Scholastics. Likewise, St. Anselm, Haymo, and St. Thomas on this passage. And then, Innocent III on Psalm 37 (38), and all more recent Latins so explain it.

From the Greeks we have in the first place Origen clearly teaching this in homily 6 in Exod. and homily 14 in Leviticus, as well as homily 12 in Jeremiah. In homily 6 in Exodus, he says: "But even to that point it is congruous, if anyone carries many good works and some little iniquity, that little bit must be melted and purged like lead in a fire, etc." Besides, Oecumenius on this passage, who also witnesses Basil's opinion, understood it to be about the purgatorial fire. St. Thomas also adds Theodoret explaining this passage in these words: "Hence we believe in the fire of purgatory, in which souls are cleansed, as gold in a crucible." (*Opisculum contra Graecos*) Gagneius relates the same teaching of Theodoret from the schools of the Greeks cited as follows: Τουτο τὸ πυρ πηςέυομεν καθαρτὴριον ἐν ᾦ καθαριζονται ἁι ψυχαι, καθά περι χρυσὶαν ἐν τῷ χωνευτηρίῳ.

But objections are made against this. *Firstly*, it is absurd that in the same sentence the Apostle would use the word fire in different ways, once for judgment and once for the purgatorial fire.

I respond to the first: we are compelled by the text itself to admit not only one, but two changes in the meaning of fire: for when he says that the day of judgment is manifested by fire, it seems he altogether speaks of the fire of conflagration; when he adds that fire will prove the work of each man, he cannot be speaking about a material fire, which cannot prove works which have passed; again, the Apostle says all works must be examined with that second fire; but with the third, not the works, but the workers are examined, and not all of them but only those who build with wood, grass and straw; necessarily the fires must be different. Still, it seems to me that what we see in the words of St. Paul is not properly an equivocation, but an elegant play on words. For, this is the sense of the whole passage: The day of the Lord will be declared by the fire of conflagration; and just as that day will be declared by fire, so the same day will be made manifest by fire, namely of the judgment of the work of every man; and just as the works will be manifested by fire, so also the workers, who need purgation, will be purged by a certain type of fire.

I say *secondly*, it is not unusual for St. Paul to use some term in different ways in the same sentence, as he receives the word "sin" in different ways when he says, "He that did not know sin became sin for us" (2 Cor. 5), and then "For sin He condemned sin." (Romans 8).

I say *thirdly*, if anyone altogether would not admit a variety of meanings, but would receive the fire everywhere for judgment, still it would not change the fact that we establish Purgatory from this passage. For then the sense would be: "If anyone's work will burn, he will suffer a detriment, but he will be saved, yet as if by fire," *i.e.*, if anyone's work cannot withstand the judgment of God, indeed the work will be condemned, but he will be saved, yet in the manner of one who has passed through the fire of divine judgment, which judgment being most just, certainly inflicted some penalty upon him.

The second objection regards the conjunction "as if" (*quasi*), which usually signifies not a truth but a similitude. *I respond*: the conjunction, *quasi*, does not mean the fire is a similitude, as if the fire were not real, but imaginary, but that the passing through is a similitude, so that the sense would be: The man that built with grass will arrive at salvation, but he will arrive in the way one arrives at some place who passes through fire, just as it is said in John 1:14, "We have seen his glory, the glory as (*quasi*) of the only begotten of the Father", *i.e.* we have seen him glorious in the manner in which it is fitting for the only begotten Son of the Father to be glorious.

CHAPTER VI
1 Corinthians 15:29

HE third passage is 1 Cor. 15:29, "What will they do, that are baptized for the dead, if the dead will not rise again? Why are they then baptized for them?" This passage clearly establishes what we want, if it is understood rightly, therefore we will briefly expound upon it. I have found six expositions of this passage.

1) The first is that the Apostle proves the coming resurrection, from the error of certain men who received Baptism in the name of some friend that had died without baptism; for they thought that just as the prayers and fasting of the living benefit the dead, so also Baptism would benefit them. Tertullian explains it this way in book 5 *in Marcionem*, as well as in his book *de Resurrectione*. Likewise, Ambrose, Anselm, and Haymo, according to which exposition prayer for the dead is gathered from this passage, because these Fathers teach that the Apostle, although he does not approve of their error, nevertheless approves of the intention which they had of helping the dead, and from this the argument is taken up: If the Apostle approves of the intention of helping the dead, certainly it cannot be condemned, nor should it be by any Christian; still, I do not think this is the true explanation.

Firstly, because the Apostle should have at least insinuated this was an error, lest he give occasion of erring. *Secondly*, because the Apostle would not have made a solid argument; for one could respond that the resurrection is not well proven from something that

Ch. VI: 1 Corinthians 15:29

certain men believed in error. For just as they erred in baptizing one for another, so they could err in believing in the future resurrection. *Thirdly*, because no ancient historian hands down that this error existed in the time of the Apostles; for Phylaster attributes this error to the Montanists who arose around 100 years after the death of St. Paul, and Chrysostom and Theophylactus attribute the same thing to the Marcionists, who began 80 years after the death of Paul; next Epiphanius (*haeresi* 28) attributes this to the Cerinthians, a sect of which arose twenty years after the death of Paul. Add that Chrysostom and Epiphanius attribute this error, not to Marcion and Cerinthus themselves, but to their posterity, and rightly so. For otherwise, how could it be that Irenaeus and Tertullian did not refute this error, who diligently refuted all the errors of Cerinthus and Marcion? Indeed, Tertullian says that this error was in the time of the Apostles, but one does not have it on any authority but his; consequently, Chrysostom and Epiphanius, as well as Theophylactus, rightly reject this explanation as false.

2) Another exposition is that the Apostle understands by "the dead" sins, when he says "they that are baptized for the dead," in other words, what will they do who are baptized for the dead, *i.e.* for washing away sins? So think Sedulius and St. Thomas on this passage of the Apostle.

On the other hand: Firstly, because the Apostle adds: "If the dead do not rise, why are they baptized for them?" undoubtedly, for dead men who do not rise; therefore he clearly teaches he is not arguing about sins, but about men. For he does not wish to show that sins rise, but that men rise. *Secondly*, because the whole force of the argument perishes if it is said, what will they do, who are baptized to wash away sins, if the dead do not rise? For the response could be made that to wash away sins is of much benefit, even if the dead do not rise, because it is good in this life to enjoy the testimony of a good conscience. Thirdly, because sins are not called dead, except when they are blotted out and extinguished, therefore Paul does not understand by "the dead" sins which still must be blotted out.

3) The third exposition is that to be baptized for the dead is simply to be baptized in the Baptism of Christ, but receiving baptism is called being baptized for the dead, because before one is baptized, one recites the Creed, which contains the article, "the resurrection of the body," so that "for the dead" means for the hope of the resurrection, or for dead bodies, *i.e.* so that in the end, our bodies which are going to die, may someday rise again immortal. So think Chrysostom, Oecumenius, and Theophylactus; but certainly this exposition is hard and violent to the text.

Firstly, because the Apostle would not have said: "What will they do who are baptized for the dead," but what will *we* do who are baptized for the dead? For everyone is baptized, not merely a few, yet the Apostle only speaks about certain men, as is clear from the form of the words as well as from what follows, "Why also are we in danger all the day?" *Secondly*, because it is unheard of that by the term "the dead" the hope of the resurrection is understood, or dead bodies, since in Greek νεκροὶ (the dead) is in the masculine gender but bodies are in the neuter gender, σώματα. *Thirdly*, because if we were said to be baptized for the dead because we recite the article on the resurrection of the dead, we could also be said to be baptized for God the Father, and for Christ and the Holy Spirit, and for the Church, because we recite all these in the Creed. *Fourthly*, because the Apostle seems altogether to understand by "the dead", dead men and nothing else, for when he says: "If the dead do not rise, why will they be baptized for them?" what can we understand by the word, *them*, except those dead who do not rise?

4) The fourth exposition is that to be baptized for the dead is to be baptized in the baptism of Christ; but Baptism is said to be for the dead because while we are baptized, we act and represent the role of one dead, while we are drowned in water, and of one rising while we rise from the water, and thus we profess the resurrection, and by this profession the Apostle proves the coming resurrection. So Theodoret and Cajetan explain it.

On the other hand, firstly because to act for something does not mean to represent it either in Hebrew, Greek or Latin, but rather to act in its place, or for its advantage. Who ever said about acting in a theater the role of Davus, or Pamphilius, that he acts *for* Davus or Pamphilus?

Secondly, because those who are baptized represent the death of Christ, and at the same time their own death, as is clear from the Apostle: "All of us who have been baptized in Christ Jesus, have been baptized into his death, for through baptism we were buried with him, etc." (Romans 6). Therefore, to be baptized for the dead will be to be baptized for oneself and for Christ, which is most absurd. The phrase to be baptized for Christ is never found in the Scripture, rather only to be baptized in Christ, or in his name, as is clear from Romans 6, Galatians 3, Acts 10 and 19.

Thirdly, because the argument of the Apostle would be null, since from the fact that one who is baptized acts the role of a dead man, it does not follow that he professes the resurrection. In that case, the Apostle would have needed to say: What will they do who are baptized for the risen, or for the dead and the risen? But even if he had said this, still it would be a trifling argument, because one could answer that in Baptism is represented the resurrection, not of the flesh from death, but of the soul from sin. For the Apostle means that in Romans 6 where he says: "That we might walk in the newness of life," and in Coloss. 3: "If you have risen with Christ, then seek those things which are above."

5) The *fifth* exposition is that of Epiphanius (*Haeresi* 28) which Peter Martyr relates, that Paul spoke about the baptism of those who were baptized in their bed, since they were *in extremis*, who formerly were called *Clinici*, and whom Cyprian jovially opposed to the Peripatetici (lib. 4, epist. 7 *ad Magnum*), namely that the *Clinici* did not walk, but remained confined to their bed, since in Greek κλινή means bed. Hence, certain men would have it that the sense of the Apostle is this: What will they do who are baptized for the dead, that is, who are baptized when they are considered more dead than alive, and when it is certain they are not baptized for any use in this life, since they are considered as dead.

This exposition is refuted *firstly*, from the words, "why are they baptized for them"? For he ought to have said, why are they baptized for *themselves*, not for them. *Secondly*, because that "for the dead" cannot be said except regarding actions which happen to the dead. *E.g.*, we rightly say he fell from a high place and was taken for dead, or he was washed and buried for dead, even if he were still living. But it is not rightly said, he walked or ate or spoke for dead. But to be baptized is of the living, not the dead, as a result, it is not rightly said that someone is baptized for dead, even if he is *in extremis*; he ought instead to be said to be baptized for living, even if he were nearly dead.

6) Consequently, the *sixth* exposition is true and germane, that the Apostle spoke about the Baptism of tears and penance, which is received by praying, fasting and almsgiving, etc. And the sense is this: "What will they do that are baptized for the dead, if the dead do not rise?" In other words, what will they do who pray, fast, weep, and afflict themselves for the dead, if the dead do not rise? St. Ephraim explains this passage in this way in his *Testamentum*, as well as Peter of Cluny in his book *Contra Petrobrusianos*, Dennis the Carthusian, Hugh of St. Victor, Gagneus and others on this passage.

This exposition is the truest. *Firstly*, because often both Scripture and the Fathers receive "to be baptized" for "to be afflicted", as in Mark 10, "Can you drink the chalice which I am going to drink, and be baptized with the baptism with which I am going to be baptized?" Or, in Luke 12: "I have a baptism to be baptized with." The fathers everywhere call the affliction of penance a laborious baptism, and a clean slate. St. Cyprian, in his sermon on the Lord's supper, says, "He baptizes himself with tears." And in the beginning of his book *de exhortatione martyrii*, he frequently calls dying for Christ a baptism. Furthermore, St. Gregory Nazianzen, in his oration *de Epiphania* says, "I know the fourth baptism which happens by martyrdom and blood, and I know the fifth of tears and penance."

Secondly, because the very punishment of purgatory is called a baptism by Scripture and the Fathers, as we read in Matthew 3, "He will baptize you with the Holy Spirit, and with fire." St. Jerome explains "with the Holy Spirit" as what takes place in this life, but by fire, what will take place in the next life. Before him St. Basil had explained the same thing in his book on the Holy Spirit, ch. 15, and after them St. Bede, commenting on ch. 3 of Luke. St. Gregory Nazianzen, in his oration *de Epiphania*, calls the fire of purgatory in another life the "last baptism". Therefore, the Apostle very neatly said that they are baptized for the dead who, afflicting themselves with prayer and fasting, take upon themselves the lot of that baptism of fire, in which souls are baptized in Purgatory.

Thirdly, this exposition especially squares with what follows: "Why also are we in danger all the day?" In other words, Why do certain men afflict themselves with prayer for the dead, and I afflict myself by preaching the Gospel, if there is no resurrection of the dead?

Fourthly, because this opinion is the same as that in 2 Maccabees 12: if the dead do not rise, it is superfluous and vain to pray for the dead.

But two arguments are made in objection to this exposition. 1) The first is that the Apostle should not have said, what will they do who are baptized for the dead, but what will we do who are baptized for the dead? For all Christians pray for the dead.

I respond: The Apostle meant to argue not by the custom of Christians, which could be rejected as a novelty by unbelievers, but by the custom of the Jews, who prayed and fasted for the dead from ancient custom and the examples in the Scriptures. In other words, what will they do, who imitating the ancient fathers, pray and fast and afflict themselves for the dead, if the dead do not rise?

2) The second argument is that it does not seem the resurrection of the dead is sufficiently proven from the fact of prayer for the dead, because therein one does not pray that they may rise, but that they may be freed from punishments, and that they might make the passage to eternal rest.

I respond: the questions on the resurrection and on the immortality of souls were so joined in the time of the Apostles, that they were considered one, as we showed above when we explained the testimony from the books of the Maccabees. Therefore, we either follow this exposition, which seems the truest to us, or the first, which is better than the other four; from which prayer for the dead is clearly gathered.

CHAPTER VII
Matthew 5:25 and Luke 12:58

HE *fourth* passage is Matthew 5 and Luke 12. "Readily consent unto your adversary while you are with him on the way lest perhaps he would hand you over to the judge, and the judge to the torturer, and you are sent into prison. Amen I say to you that you will not go out from there until you pay the last farthing." Here we must explain what are the road, the adversary, the judge, the torturer, the prison, and lastly the farthing.

On the *first*, Chrysostom teaches on Matthew 5 that the way is properly understood as a real road on which one journeys to a judge in this world; for Chrysostom thinks this is no parable, but that the Lord means this literally so as to terrify the anxious with the threat of human danger, so that the judge is understood to be a man, the torturer a man, the prison a physical prison of this life, and the farthing a real golden coin. Ochinus contends that the passage must be explained in this way. I have two things to say in response to this.

In the first place, it is simply not probable, not only because it is opposed to all the other expositors (Origen, Cyprian, Hilary, Ambrose, Jerome, Augustine, Bede, Anselm and the more recent ones, such as Abulensis, Lyranus, Cajetan, Jansen and others), who teach that the road means the present life, just as when it is said: "Blessed are the immaculate on the road" (Psalm. 118/119), and they consider this discourse to be for the most part metaphorical. Besides that, the Lord does not usually teach and instruct human prudence in earnest, since he often witnessed that the sons of this age are more prudent than the sons of light. Moreover, the Lord would not have so definitively said: "Amen I say to you, you will not go out from there until you have paid the last farthing," if he were speaking of a human judge, since we often see that the contrary happens and the guilty are freed because they have the favor of someone, or they escape, and pay nothing.

Secondly, I say that if we must consider the opinion of Chrysostom probable, it can only be accepted for the words as found in Matthew 5:25 which he explains. In regard to the words of Luke 12:58, by no means can it be accepted, for as Ambrose rightly noted, the Lord spoke these words twice, different occasions having been offered. For in Matthew 5 he spoke these words when he was speaking about the love of enemies and on bearing injuries, and therefore the exposition of Chrysostom can be tolerated to that extent. But in Luke 12 the Lord speaks about the future judgment, for he says: "Gird your loins." And then, "Watch, because at an hour you think not, the Lord will come." And at the end he concludes: "Therefore, when you go with your adversary to the Prince," where he clearly shows that he speaks about the future judgment, which will take place after this life; which is also confirmed from what he says right before this: "Why do you not judge for yourselves what is just? For, when you go with your adversary, etc." For he intends to admonish them, this parable being taken from what men usually do; for debtors normally expend every labor to free themselves from a creditor before it comes to trial. This is why Theophylactus and Euthymius, who follow Chrysostom on

Matthew 5, nevertheless on Luke 12 rightly say that life is meant by the way, and God by the judge, etc.

On the second, even if it makes little difference who the adversary might be and delays our thesis on purgatory, nevertheless, since it is a worthy matter to discover, we will explain it briefly. Some men understand the adversary to be the devil, such as Origen (hom. 35 in Luke), Ambrose, Euthymius, and Theophylactus (in c. 12 of Luke) as well as Jerome in epistle 8 to Demetriadis. Jerome does not rebuke this opinion in his commentary on Matthew 5 when he says: "Certain men explain it with an even more forced interpretation, etc." For that "more forced", is an error of the printers, and ought to be read "more cautious".

You might ask how we ought to consent to the devil when on the contrary we are bid to resist him? Jerome responds that we ought to consent to him insofar as we are held to stand in the pact initiated with him in Baptism. For then we renounced the devil and his pomps, but if we again desire and take possession of his pomps, which we have renounced, he will rightly accuse us before the Lord. This opinion is not very probable, and is refuted by Augustine (lib. 1 *de Sermone Domini in monte*, c. 22) for the Greek is ἐυνοῶν, that is, *friendly and harmonious*, but we cannot be friends with the devil; next, when he desires that we lust for his pomps, and tempts us for this purpose, then we should be consenting to him, if we were to desire his pomps and would offend God.

Others explain by the adversary, the flesh, but this is rightly refuted by Augustine, since it cannot be commanded to the spirit to consent to the flesh, since this would be a sin. Others understand the spirit as the adversary, to which the flesh is bid to consent. Jerome refutes this, because it is not credible that the spirit is going to hand over its own flesh to the judge; nor will the flesh go into prison without the spirit, but either the spirit alone, or the spirit and flesh together. Others, by adversary, at least in Luke, understand sin because Luke says: "Labor by every means to be freed from him." Ambrose thinks thus, but it is not probable, for to be freed from the adversary is not to flee from or extinguish him, but to settle up with him, which is clear both from Matthew and from the word ἀντίδικος, namely a litigant or a plaintiff. Others understand by adversary another man, who evidently has harmed us, or we him. Hilary, Anselm and Jerome argue this from Matthew 5, and although it is probable, at least in regard to the text of Matthew 5, nevertheless, Augustine refutes it (*loc. cit.*). *Firstly*, because it seems that here the Lord speaks about an adversary that is always with us on the way, and with whom we can always make an agreement as long as the road endures: but a human adversary often dies before his adversary and deserts him on the road. Nor yet may it be said that the just man who is on the road cannot be saved by repentance, if he cannot come to an agreement with his adversary.

Secondly, because properly speaking one man does not hand another to God the judge; or at least there are many other things which are more properly said to hand one over, as we will say, especially because the Greek is ἀντίδικος, which does not mean an adversary by reason of injury but of a lawsuit, that is a plaintiff or an accuser.

Consequently, the truest exposition is that the adversary is the law of God, or God himself, insofar as he commands things contrary to the flesh, or the conscience, which always objects the law of God to the sinner, since these nearly coincide in the same thing. Thus Ambrose, Bede, and Bonaventure (in c. 12 of Luke) explain it. Likewise, St. Anselm and St. Augustine on Matthew 5, and also the same Augustine in hom. 1 *de verbis Domini*, hom. 5 in his book of 50 sermons, and in his book *de decem chordis c. 3*, St. Gregory hom. 39, and Bernard, serm. 85 *in Cantica*. For the law of God and our conscience are always with us on the road, always opposed to wicked desires, and it is of great advantage to be at peace with them, and to be freed from their enmity; at worst they will be accusers and witnesses against us in the judgment.

There seems to be only one obstacle to this exposition, which is that in Matthew 5 just before this parable the Lord was speaking on reconciliation with a human adversary.

I respond: After the Lord taught that man ought to be reconciled with man, he meant to advise with this parable that we must also remember to be reconciled with God or with his law. Besides, even if it is probable on account of this reason that in Matthew 5 the adversary is understood to be a man, nevertheless, in Luke 12 we cannot understand anything but the law of God, or conscience. This is why Cajetan, who explains Matthew 5 to be on a man, explains Luke 12 to be on conscience.

On the third, all agree that the judge is Christ, since the Scriptures everywhere teach this and especially John 5: "The Father has given all judgment to the son."

On the fourth, Ambrose (in c. 12 of Luke) as well as Augustine (lib. 1 *de serm. Domini in monte*, c. 21) understand by ministers, the good angels. St. Gregory (homil. 39) and Theophylactus, on Luke 12, understand the demons; both opinions are probable.

On the fifth, all likewise agree that the jail is hell, in which there are many mansions, some for the damned, others for those who are purged. Formerly the most absurd heresy of Carpocratis stood out, as Irenaeus relates (l. 1 c. 24), who said everyone should be exercised in every type of punishment, and therefore souls going out from the body, as if from prison, are examined by the judge, and unless they had suffered all tortures, they would be remitted to another body just like a prison, and this would happen as many times as needed until they had altogether passed through every torment; and he thought the Lord meant this when he said: "You will not go out from there until you pay the last farthing." But this opinion is too absurd to be worth refuting.

On the sixth, nearly everyone also agrees that by the last farthing petty sins are understood, for the farthing is the smallest coin. For what Augustine says, that the last farthing means earthly sins, because earth is the final element, seems very hard and forced, because still the Lord does not mean to say one must merely pay a farthing, but the whole debt even to the last farthing. There remains a doubt, however, whether this payment is made in hell or in purgatory? Augustine thinks it is a question of the eternal punishments of hell and therefore he says that "Until you pay," does not mean a certain time, but eternity, like when it is said in Matthew 1: "He did not know her until she gave birth to her son." And in Psalm 109: "Sit at my right, until I place your enemies as your footstool." And in 1 Cor. 15: "He must uphold heaven until all are subjected beneath his feet."[6] But one may not gather therefore that after Mary gave birth Joseph knew her, and so on for the rest.

Others, such as Albert the Great and Cajetan, explain it about hell and purgatory together, so that the sense would be: If the debt is unpayable, you will never go out; if it is payable, you will go out when you have paid everything exactly. Others understand it to be only on purgatory, namely those whom we will cite in a moment.

This third opinion is the truest of all. It is proved: 1) Because the most ancient fathers understood this passage in this way. Tertullian (*de Anima*, c. 17), "...he commits you to the prison of hell, from where you will not be dismissed unless even your smallest offense has been paid off during the time before the resurrection." Note there, he must only remain in the prison of purgatory to the end, up to the resurrection.

Cyprian, (lib. 4, epist. 2) says: "They are two different things, to stand for pardon and arrive at glory; to be sent into prison to not go out from it until one pays the last penny, and right away to receive the reward for faith and virtue; to be freed from sins after a long period of torture, and to be purged for a while in fire, and at the last to have purged all sins by martyrdom." (see above, ch. 5)

Origen (hom. 35 in Lucam) says: "But if we owe a great deal of money, like that man of whom it is written that he owed ten thousand talents, I cannot clearly say how long

---

[6] Translator's note: The Vulgate Bellarmine uses has: *"Oportet illum coelum suscipere, donec omnia subjiciantur pedibus ejus."* The subsequent revision has: *"Oportet autem illum regnare donec ponat omnes inimocos sub pedibus ejus,"* "He must reign until he shall place all enemies under his feet."

Ch. VII: Matthew 5:25 and Luke 12:58

we will be shut up in prison. For if a man who owes a little will not go out until he pays the smallest farthing, then certainly someone that is liable to such a debt will have centuries numbered for him to repay." And on the Epistle to the Romans he says: "Although he is promised to go out from the prison at some point, nevertheless, it is indicated that he cannot go out from there until he shall pay the last penny."

Eusebius Emissenus, or rather Caesarius of Arles, or whoever was the author of these homilies, (hom. 3 *de Epiphania*) says: "But these men, who have acted so as to be worthy of temporal punishments, to whom God has so directed his pronouncements that they do not go out from there until they have paid the last farthing, will pass through the fiery river, etc."

Ambrose, explaining this passage in chapter 12 of Luke, says: "We recall that a farthing is usually given in the baths, the offering of which is made so that each man that pays receives the opportunity to wash there; so here he receives the opportunity to wash. because each man's sin is washed by the kind of situation described, although for a long time the guilty man is trained by punishments to pay the penalties of the error committed."

Jerome on chapter 5 of Matthew says: "This is what he says, you will not go out from prison until you have satisfied also for the smallest sins." Bernard (*serm. de obitu Huberti*), says: "Know this, for after this life in the confines of purgatory you will pay a hundred fold for the things which were neglected here, even to the last penny."

Secondly, it is proved because it does not seem possible to rightly say, "Until you shall pay the last penny," unless at some point there will be an end of the payment. The examples of St. Augustine do not satisfy, for when it is said: "He did not know her until she gave birth," it is indeed not lawful to infer that therefore, later he did, but it is lawful to infer that therefore, she gave birth at some point. Likewise, when it is said: "Sit at my right until I will place, etc." it is rightly inferred that therefore at some point all the enemies of Christ will be put beneath his feet; otherwise that: "*Until*" would be said ineptly. So therefore when it is said: "You will not go out until you have paid the last farthing," we rightly infer: Thus at some point he will pay the last farthing, and consequently he will go out from there.

Thirdly, it is proven from the foundation and scope of this parable; for the similitude is not taken from a murderer or adulterer, or traitor, who are condemned to death, or to life in prison, or to be a galley slave, but from a debtor who, not on account of a crime, but on account of a monetary debt is thrown into prison until he pays. And men of this sort ordinarily go out after some time, as is clear. Therefore the scope of the parable is that in this life we should settle with God, when we can easily obtain the remission of the penalty due for our sins, nor should we wait for a future age, in which it will be exacted severely. That is all for this passage.

CHAPTER VIII
Matthew 5:22, Luke 16:9, Luke 23:42, Acts 2:24 and Philippians 2:10.

HE FIFTH passage is Matthew 5. "Anyone that is angry with his brother will be liable to judgment, and he who says to his brother, racha, will be liable to the Council, he who says 'you fool,' will be liable to the Gehenna of fire." Note here the discussion is certainly on the punishment enjoined in the court of God, as is clear from that: "he will be liable to the Gehenna of fire." This is why St. Augustine (lib. 1 *de serm. Domini in monte,* cap. 19) explains all three as referring to the penalties for souls after this life. Note *secondly,* that it is also certain that here three kinds of sins and penalties are distinguished, as Augustine explains in the same place, and eternal damnation is only given for the third kind of sin, *i.e.* for crimes. But for others inasmuch as they are lighter sins, lighter punishments are given, and hence temporal ones. From that it is inferred that some souls after this life are punished with temporal punishments.

Someone might say, but Christ said: He that kills will be liable to judgment, thus, to be liable to judgment is to be condemned to hell, for murder is a lethal crime. *I respond:* When the Lord says: "It was said to the ancients, he who murders shall be liable to judgment," he speaks about human and temporal judgment, whereby murderers are punished with temporal death; for the old law threatens murderers with no other death, as is clear from Exodus 21. So the Lord meant to say that homicide is punished by death in this world, but in the next life the agitation of internal anger, although it is a venial sin, is punished with a certain penalty which is indeed temporal, but which is equal with temporal death; and anger protruding outwardly is punished still more severely; but a contumelious word, and murder much more so, is punished with eternal death.

Someone might insist: Granted, the Lord speaks in this passage on the penalties to be inflicted by the judgment of God, still, it does not follow that there are temporal punishments in another life; for God can inflict punishments of this sort in this life.

I answer *firstly*, this passage is understood by Augustine and other fathers to be about penalties after this life. *Secondly,* I say, from this passage it can be deduced that at least some purgatorial punishments take place after this life, for hence we have it that certain sins do not merit anything but a temporal penalty, but it can happen that someone might die with such sins, for one can die suddenly, or while sleeping, so that he would have no space for penance. Therefore, in the next life he will be purged, otherwise either he will go into heaven tainted or unjustly be condemned to eternal punishments, when he did not merit anything but temporal punishments.

The sixth passage is Luke 16: Make friends for yourselves from the mammon of iniquity so that when you falter, they might receive you in the eternal dwellings." For falter (*deficere*) all understand to die; for *friends*, they understand the saints who reign with Christ, from which it follows that men are helped after death by the prayers of the saints.

Yet, because someone could say that here it is a question of the virtue of almsgiving and the sense is, those

Chapter VIII: Matt. 5, Luke 16, Luke 23, Acts 2, Phil. 2

who gives alms, when they die are saved on account of the good works they did, it must be observed that not only does the Lord mean this, but also he means that after death souls are aided by the prayers of the saints. 1) For this purpose they bring forth the words: "Make friends ... so that they will receive you." For almsgiving which is made to wicked men, yet with a good intention, is meritorious, but nevertheless does not make friends who could receive you in the eternal dwellings. This is why St. Jerome (at the end of his book *Contra Vigilantium*), says that the Lord exhorts us to give alms more to the good than the bad, so that those who give alms might be saved by the intercession of good men. Ambrose argues in like manner on this passage, as well as St. Augustine (lib. 21 *de civitate Dei*, c. 27), and they say that by friends the saints reigning with Christ are understood, who help us with their prayers, and will help us when we die.

2) The similitude itself compels us to this conclusion, for the parable was taken from a certain steward who was deposed from office, and having become poor and needy implored help of his friends; and that in the application of the parable to be deposed from office is to die, the Lord himself explains.

3) Add that Augustine (*loc. cit.*) proves purgatory from this passage, for he says there are some so holy that they fly straight to heaven after death and who are not only saved themselves, but can also help others; again certain others are so bad that they can neither help themselves nor be helped by others, but descend to eternal punishments without a remedy. Then, there are some in the middle who die in such a state that they are neither worthy of eternal death, nor do their own merits suffice for them to enter

unto salvation, namely to be received right away into heaven, and these, he says, are the ones that are received into the eternal dwellings by the prayers of their friends.

Peter Martyr has no response to this passage, but objects to himself in the name of Catholics, the words that follow after this parable, and he says that we assert the rich man was in purgatory since he asked assistance of Abraham, and he painstakingly answers this argument as if it were our Achilles, and at the same time deduces from there that souls cannot be aided by the living, seeing that neither Abraham nor Lazarus could help the rich man. Peter Martyr jokingly wonders why the rich man did not also seek to have Mass said for him on his anniversary. But nearly all Catholics say that the rich man is in hell, hence Peter Martyr is fighting the wind.

The seventh passage is Luke 23:42, "Remember me when you come into your kingdom." The good man, instructed by the Holy Spirit, would never have said this unless he believed that after this life his sins could be forgiven, and that souls need help and can be helped. Certainly, St. Augustine proves from here that some sins are remitted after death. (*Julian.* lib. 6, c. 5).

The eighth passage is Acts 2:24, "The man whom God has raised up, having loosed the pains of hell, because it was impossible that he be held by them." St. Augustine understands this passage to mean that when Christ descended to hell, he freed many from the tortures of hell, which since it cannot be understood about the damned, seems necessarily to be understood of those who were being purged (epist. 99 ad Evodium; Gen. l. 12, c. 33). Epiphanius also upholds this in his relation of the heresy of Tatian, which is the last of the first book. There,

Chapter VIII: Matt. 5, Luke 16, Luke 23, Acts 2, Phil. 2

Epiphanius said that when Christ descended to hell he freed those who had sinned by ignorance but had not departed from the faith of God. And apart from the authority of these Fathers, it is proven from the very words of Scripture. The phrase, "having loosed the pains of hell," cannot be understood about the pains of Christ himself, since the pains of Christ were completed on the cross, as is clear from the words of Luke 23:43, "Today you will be with me in paradise." It is also not about the pains of the damned, which is clear because they have been condemned to the eternal flames. It is also not about the sufferings of the holy fathers, for they suffered no pains, as Augustine teaches (*loc. cit.*) and also St. Gregory the Great (hom. 22). Therefore, it remains that this passage refers to the sorrows of the souls of Purgatory.

But someone will say the Greeks do not read, "having loosed the pains of hell," rather, having loosed the pains of death, το θανάτου, not τοῦ ἅδου.

I respond: Firstly, the ancient Latin vulgate edition is with us. *Secondly*, the Syriac, which reads likewise: "God raised him and loosed the ropes of hell." *Thirdly*, the most ancient fathers, both Greek and Latin, for St. Polycarp, at the beginning of his epistle, citing this passage, writes: "having loosed the pains of hell." Likewise, St. Cyprian (Serm. *de cœna Domini*, at the beginning), looks to this passage and says: "But the pious teacher willed to show it was impossible for his soul to be detained by hell." Epiphanius and also Augustine, without a doubt, read the verse in this way. Next, it is proven from the following words, for Peter proves what he had said from Psalm 15 (16): "You will not leave my soul in hell, nor will you allow your holy one to see corruption."

The ninth passage is Philippians 2:10, "That at the name of Jesus every knee should bend, in heaven, on the earth and in hell." St. Augustine uses this passage (*de Gen.* lib. 12, c. 33) although it is not improbable that "in hell," refers to demons. Similar to this is that passage in Apocalypse 5: "Who is worthy to open the book and break its seven seals? And no one was found in heaven, or on the earth, or under the earth." By those who are in heaven angels are understood, by those who are on the earth, just men, by those who are under the earth, none can be understood except the souls of purgatory, for this is not attributed to the damned. And the fathers who had been in limbo had already been liberated.

Our own use this passage, but it does not seem to carry much weight; for it is probable that for those who are under the earth the fathers who were in limbo could be understood, for even if when John wrote this the fathers had gone out from limbo, still they had not gone out at the time of which he is speaking. He speaks about a time which preceded the death of Christ, therefore he adds: "The Lion from the tribe of Juda, the root of David, has prevailed to open the book, etc." For Christ, by his death, opened the mysteries of the book which had been closed even to that day. Likewise, that which is asserted in the same chapter, where creatures who are in heaven, and on the earth and who are under the earth are said to have given praise to God, does not convince, for here, by creatures inanimate things could be understood such as fire, and hail, etc., which in Psalm 148 are invited to praise God, especially since John adds even those which are in the sea.

CHAPTER IX
Purgatory is Asserted in the Testimonies of Councils

HE *second* argument is taken from Councils and the custom of the Church. In the first place, what the African Church thought is clear from the third Council of Carthage, c. 29: "And the sacraments of the altar are not celebrated except by men that fast, but if the commendation of some dead men is to be made in the afternoon, let it be done with prayers only." You can see similar things in the fourth Council of Carthage, c. 79.

The Spanish Church thought the same thing, as is clear from the first Council of Braga, cap. 34, where it commands that prayers should not be offered for those that committed suicide. In chapter 39 it is commanded that the offerings made should be divided among the clerics so that they might pray for the dead.

The French Church thought the same, as is clear from the Council of Cabilonense (Chalon-sur-Saôn), in *de consecr.* dist. 1, Canon *Visum est*: "Besides, it has been seen that in all solemn rites of Masses in church the Lord is beseeched for the spirits of the dead in a fitting place." See also the second Council of Arles, cap. 14.

The German Church thought the same thing, as is clear from the Council of Worms, c. 10, where it is defined that prayer and sacrifice must be offered even for those that are hanged.

The Italian Church thought the same, as is clear from the sixth Council under Symmachus, where it is said to be a sacrilege to cheat the souls of the dead of prayers.

The Greek Church thought the same, as it is clear from the Council of the Greeks gathered under the Bishop Martin of Bracarens (can. 69). Nay more, some Greeks seem even to have wanted to help the souls of the dead too much, for in the 3rd Council of Constantinople, can. 83, those who tried to force the Holy Eucharist into the mouths of those who had died without holy communion are rebuked.

Next, we add the general Councils of the whole Church: Lateran III under Pope Innocent (c. 66), Florence, in its last session, in the decree on Purgatory, and the Council of Trent in its 25th session, in the beginning, and all the liturgies, that of James, Basil, Chrysostom, Ambrose, etc. For in all prayer is made for the dead.

Peter Martyr responds with three arguments, in the place we already cited.

1) He says: "It is usually objected to us that the Church has always prayed for the dead, and I do not deny this. Yet, I declare that this deed has authority neither from the word of God, nor from an example which is taken from the sacred letters. Men are easily moved by an impulse of a certain natural charity, and love for the dead, to wish them well, and they break out into some prayers for them. But this very forceful affection appears to be opposed to faith and just piety." With these words Peter Martyr argues against the whole Church, that it prays for the dead without the testimony of Scripture, and that it does this from a very forceful affection toward the dead, which is opposed to faith and piety.

a) St. Augustine suffices for the *first* part of the accusation in his book *De Cura pro Mortuis*, c. 1, where he says: "You add that one cannot be unacquainted with the

Ch. IX: Purgatory proven from Councils 79

fact that the universal Church customarily prays for the dead" And below, approving this opinion of St. Paulinus, to whom he writes: "In the books of the Maccabees, we read that a sacrifice was offered for the dead, but even if no such thing were read at all in the Old Testament Scriptures, the authority of the universal Church, which is well known for this custom, is no small thing; where during the prayers of the priest which are poured forth to God at his altar, the commendation of the dead also has its place."

b) We can easily respond to the *second* part of the accusation. What arises from natural affection in prayers for the dearly departed, even if someone thought they did not benefit them at all, can happen in private prayers as well as those which are recited spontaneously, but how could that happen in the solemn prayers of the Church which are read from a book, and have been composed with mature judgment and approved by a Council of Bishops?

c) St. Paul satisfies *the third* part when he says: "The Church is the pillar and firmament of truth." (1 Timothy 3). Also St. Augustine, who says in epistle 118, that to dispute against that which the universal Church does is the most insolent insanity. Next, reason itself, for if the universal Church can be opposed to true faith and just piety, as Peter Martyr says, therefore the whole Church can fall to ruin, against the explicit prophecy of Christ in Matthew 16:18: "The gates of hell will not prevail against it." Which is more believable, that the universal Church could fall to ruin and Christ and Paul lied, or, Peter Martyr labors in the most insolent insanity? I leave that to the judgment of any sane man.

2) *The second* answer of Peter Martyr is that the Church does not pray for the dead so that it might free them from Purgatory, but so as to preserve for itself a witness of their memory, and to also preserve as richly as it can. "And the Church may have made prayers for the dead for other reasons besides purgatory. For they did not want the name of the dead and their memory to perish so easily." But St. Augustine treats this question in *De Cura pro Mortuis*, ch. 1, whether the prayers of the Church benefit the souls of the dead, and he says they benefit those who were not very wicked in this life, and who merited so as to benefit themselves; but not those that were very wicked and hence merited nothing such as this. Hence, the imagination of Peter Martyr is answered.

3) The third response is that the Church merely exercised its office toward the dead, as if they were still living, and therefore it asked for them that which it thought that they already attained, in the way that Christ prayed for the raising of Lazarus, even though he knew that he already received what he asked for. St. Ambrose, in his prayer on the death of Theodosius congratulates him because he already reigned with Christ, and still at that very instant he prays for him that God would concede to him the rest he desired. Epiphanius (*haeresi* 75), says they pray even for the holy Patriarchs, Prophets, Apostles and Martyrs.

I respond: If that were so the Church would pray for all equally, even for Martyrs; but it does not do this. As Augustine says (*Tract. in Joan.* 84), "Therefore, we do not commemorate martyrs at the altar, as we do other dead who rest in peace, so as to pray for them, but rather so that they would pray for us."

Nor does it appear to fit in any way that someone asks for what he already has; when Christ prayed for Lazarus, he had not yet received what he asked, as Lazarus had still not risen. It is one thing to ask for that which we know we are going to receive, and another to ask for that which we have already received. Furthermore, Ambrose hoped that Theodosius was already in heaven, and therefore rejoiced for him, and at the same time, because he did not know for certain whether this was so, he prayed for him. Epiphanius in truth does not say anywhere that in the Church the saints are prayed for, but he does say that the commemoration of all the faithful departed is made in the Church, both of sinners and of the just, and he adds: "of sinners," that we might implore mercy for them from God and, "of the just", so that we might distinguish them from Christ.

But we distinguish the saints from Christ not, as Peter Martyr says, because we pray for the saints, and not for Christ, but because we offer the sacrifice of thanksgiving for the saints; whereas we do not offer it for Christ, but rather to Christ with the Father and the Holy Spirit, which can be understood from the Greek liturgy about which Epiphanius speaks, and which is extent in volume 5 of Chrysostom. There the commemoration is made of all the saints, and it is said: "We offer to you, O Lord, the sacrifice for the Patriarchs, Apostles, Prophets, Martyrs, and especially the most blessed Theotokos." But that this sacrifice is not offered for their sins, but for their glory, is clear, for the liturgy immediately adds: "And remember all the faithful departed who have fallen asleep in the hope of the resurrection, and let them rest where the light of your countenance is seen." The same thing can be understood from Augustine (tract. 84 in *Ioan.*), and from St. Cyril of Jerusalem (*Catech.* 5, Mystagogica), and from our liturgy, which is altogether the same sort of thing which Cyril, Epiphanius and Augustine describe.

CHAPTER X
Purgatory is Asserted in the Testimonies of the Greek and Latin Fathers

HE first of the Fathers, Clement (lib. 8 *const.* c. 48), describes a long oration customarily said for the dead. Dionysius (*de Ecclesiast. Hierarch,* c. 7, par. 3) said, "Then the venerable Bishop approaching carries out the sacred prayer for the dead; that prayer asks for divine mercy so that he might forgive all the sins committed by the dead man through human frailty, and place him in the light, and the land of the living." Athanasius, or whoever is the author of q. 34 *ad Antiochum*, asks whether souls perceive an advantage from the prayers of the living? He answers that they altogether do. Basil instituted prayer for the dead in his *Liturgy*.

Gregory Nazianzen (*Oratione in Caesarium*) says: "We commend to the same God our souls and theirs, who like those more prepared on the road arrive at their lodging earlier." In the same oration he prays for the soul of the Emperor. St. Ephraim says in his *Testamentum*: "Continually remember me in your prayers, for truly I lived my life in vanity and iniquity."

Cyril, in Catechesis 5, *Mystagogica,* says: "Next, we pray for all those who have lived among us, believing this to be of great assistance to those souls for whom the supplication of this holy and awesome sacrifice is offered." Eusebius (lib. 4 *de vita Constantini*), says that Constantine wanted to be buried in a famous Church so that he could be made a partaker of many prayers. Epiphanius, at the end of his work against heresies, numbers prayer for the dead among the dogmas of the Church, and in *haeresi* 75 he says Aërius was a heretic because he denied this.

Chrysostom (hom. 41 on 1 Corinthians) says: "The dead are assisted not with tears but prayers, supplications and almsgiving... Let us not tire of bringing aid to the dead, offering prayers for them." Again in homily 69 he says: "The commemoration of the dead that is made in the awesome mysteries was not rashly ratified by the Apostles, for they knew that from it they obtain much fruit and profit." He says the same thing in other places (hom. 32 in Matth., and 84 in John, hom. 3 in epist. ad Philipp., and 21 in Acts of the Apostles). Theodoret writes that Theodosius the younger laid prostrate before the relics of St. John Chrysostom and prayed for the souls of his parents Arcadius and Eudoxia that had recently died (lib. 5 *hist.* c. 26).

Theophylactus (in cap. 12 Luc.) said: "I say this on account of the sacrifices and distributions which are made for the dead, which bring no small benefit, even to those who died in grave crimes." St. John Damascene, in his book on those that had died in faith, proves this truth with many testimonies of Dionysius, Athanasius, Gregory Nazianzen, Gregory of Nyssa, and others. See also Palladius in *historia Lausiaca*, cap. 41.

Now let us come to the Latins. Tertullian in *de Corona*, numbers suffrage for the dead among the Apostolic traditions, and in his book *de Monogamia* he says: "Let her pray for his [the dead spouse's] soul, and beg for him refreshment in the meanwhile, and to be a partaker in the first resurrection, and offer sacrifices on the anniversaries of his death, for unless she will do these things, truly she repudiates him, so far as it lies in her." He says the same thing in his book *de exhortatione castitatis*.

St. Cyprian (lib. 1 epist. 9), says: "Our predecessor Bishops decreed that no brother at the point of death shall name a cleric as a trustee for his last will and testament, but if anyone were to do this then no offering will be made for him, nor will the sacrifice be celebrated on the anniversary of his death... And therefore Victor, since against the form recently given by the priests in a Council, he has dared to constitute Geminius Faustinus, a priest, as his trustee, is not one for whose eternal rest you will make an offering, or any prayer."

St. Ambrose (l. 2 ep. 8 ad Faustinum *de obitu sororis*): "Therefore, I reckon that her soul is not so much to be lamented as to be escorted with prayers, nor to be mourned with your tears, but rather to be commended to God with sacrifices." See also the orations on the death of Theodosius, on the death of Valentinian and on the death of Satyrus, in all of which he prays to God for the souls of the aforesaid, and promises that he will offer sacrifices for them.

St. Jerome, in an epistle to Pammachius on the death of his wife Paulina, says: "Other husbands scatter violets, roses, lilies and purple flowers over the tombs of their wives; our Pammachius waters her holy ashes and venerable bones with the sweet balsam of almsgiving. With these spices and perfumes he keeps her ashes at rest, knowing that it is written: As *water extinguishes fire, so also almsgiving sin.*"

St. Paulinus of Nola, in an epistle to the same Pammachius, praises him because he had satisfied for both the body and soul of his deceased wife, her body by tears, her soul by almsgiving. The same saint says in epistle 5 to a Bishop named Delphinus, commending to him the soul of his brother: "See to it that by your prayers he might receive pardon, and from the least finger of your holiness the trickling drops of eternal rest might sprinkle his soul." And, in the following epistle, which is the first to Amandus, he says similar things, commending the same soul to the Bishop Amandus.

St. Augustine says in his book *de cura pro mortuis*, ch. 2: "In the books of the Maccabees, we read that a sacrifice was offered for the dead, but even if no such thing were read at all in the Old Testament Scriptures, the authority of the universal Church, which is well known for this custom, is no small thing; where in the prayers of the priest which are poured forth to God at his altar, the commendation of the dead also has its place." And in ch. 4: "So, when the mind recollects where the body of a very dear friend lies buried, and thereupon there occurs to the thoughts a place rendered venerable by the name of a martyr, to that same martyr it commends the soul in affection of heartfelt recollection and prayer. And when this affection is shown to the departed by faithful men who were most dear to them, there is no doubt that it profits them... Supplications for the spirits of the dead are not to be omitted: which supplications, that they should be made for all that die in Christian and Catholic communion, even without mentioning of their names, under a general commemoration, the Church has received, so that they who have not parents or sons or whatever kindred or friends to pray for them, may have the same afforded unto them by the one pious mother which is common to all." (You can see the same thing in the following: *Enchirid.* c.

110, lib. 9; *Confessiones*, c. 13; Sermon *de verbis Apostoli*, 17 and 34; *de Civitate Dei*, lib. 21, ch. 24; *in Joann.* tract. 84, q. 2; *ad Dulcitium*, and at length, *de haeresibus*, c. 53, where he makes Aërius a heretic because he denied that sacrifices must be offered for the dead).

St. Gregory the Great (Dial., lib. 4, cap. 55) says: "The sacred offering of the salutary host customarily assists souls even after death, so that sometimes the souls of the dead themselves seem to demand this." And in ch. 50 he says: "It benefits the dead who are not weighed down by serious sins if they are buried in the Church, because their neighbors, as often as they gather in the same sacred places, see their sepulchers, remember them, and pour forth prayers to the Lord for them."

Isidore (lib. 1 *de officiis divinis*, c. 18) says: "Unless the Catholic Church believed that sins are remitted to the faithful departed, she would not give alms or offer Mass to God for their spirits." Victor (*de perseq. Wandal.*, lib. 2) says: "Who of us that are dying will be buried with the solemn prayers?"

Lastly, St. Bernard (serm. 66 in *Cantica*,), and Peter of Cluny (in lib. *contra Petrobrusianos*) have written against this error directly. St. Malachi as quoted by Bernard says: "No small hope is laid up for me for that day, in which such benefits are bestowed upon the dead by the living."

But it will be worthwhile to listen to what Calvin and Peter Martyr should say in response. Peter Martyr answers that nearly all the fathers erred in some matter, and he enumerates their errors. But they erred in private opinions which others refuted; they cannot all agree at the same time in one error, otherwise the universal Church would err and perish.

But Calvin says four things in *The Institutes*, book 3, ch. 5 §10.

1) *Firstly* he says: "1300 years ago the custom was received of offering prayers for the dead." And after interposing some remarks he adds: "But I declare they were all carried off into error." This confession is certainly enough to condemn Calvin, for how is it believable that the Church persisted in such a crass error for 1300 years and there was not one of the ancients who resisted it, with the exception of Aërius, whom both we and the Calvinists hold for a heretic?

2) *Secondly*, he says the ancients prayed for the dead not in order to help them, but to show pious affection for them and to console themselves. But this is a lie since clearly the cited fathers say it helps souls, and they distinguish the solace of the living from the help conferred upon the dead, especially St. Augustine in *Enchiridion*, c. 110 and throughout his book *de Cura pro Mortuis*.

3) *Thirdly*, he says the common Christian people began to pray for the dead out of imitation of the gentiles, and moreover, the Fathers accommodated themselves to the opinion of the flock, as is clear from Augustine, in his book *de Cura pro mortuis*, where he especially argues on this matter. In regard to this, Calvin says, "He disputes so doubtfully, hesitatingly and tepidly, that by his chill he could extinguish the zeal of those defending Purgatory. He prayed what he did for his mother because he did not examine the womanish wish of his mother by the Scriptures, and wanted to approve of all this from a certain private emotion."

But this is also a lie, for in the first place there was never anyone more diligent than the Fathers in forbidding pagan rites, especially when many pagans were converting. Certainly Tertullian and Cyprian were most severe castigators of every pagan superstition, so much so that Tertullian bitterly rebuked Christian soldiers who wore a crown in the custom of heathen soldiers, yet even they urged prayer for the dead. Besides, the Fathers not only do not rebuke this custom, but even decide in their Councils that it must be done, and urge it to be done, and lead the way by their own example, and finally many of them say this is Apostolic tradition, and number Aërius among the heretics for teaching the contrary. What more could they say? Furthermore, St. Augustine, in his book *de Cura pro Mortuis*, ch. 4, precisely says that there is no doubt that souls are assisted, and in the whole book there is not one syllable which would insinuate the slightest doubt, of which Calvin speaks. Moreover, that he calls St. Monica's wish "old womanish", and blames St. Augustine for taking care to fulfill it, is no wonder, since Calvin customarily rebukes and ridicules the saints.

4) *Fourthly*, he says that the Fathers never asserted anything precisely on purgatory, so they held it for an uncertain matter. But this is also an intolerable impudence, or else ignorance. In the first place, even if they had never used the word Purgatory, nevertheless, what the Fathers thought about it could be sufficiently understood from the fact that they so clearly taught that the souls of certain faithful need rest and are helped by the prayers of the living.

Next, there are the clearest passages in the Fathers where they assert purgatory, a few of which I will cite here.

Gregory of Nyssa, in his oration for the dead, says: "Either having been purged in the present life by prayers and the study of wisdom, or after death having made expiation in the furnace of the purging fire, he willed to return to original happiness ... After going out from the body he will not be able to be made a partaker of divinity unless the purgatorial fire takes away the stains intermixed with his soul. ... While others wipe away their stains by a material purgatorial fire after this life."

Ambrose, on the words of Psalm 36, "Sinners unsheathed their sword," says: "Even if the Lord will save his servants, we will be saved by faith, yet so saved as if by fire. Even if we are not burned up, still we are burned. Yet how some remain in the fire, while others pass through, let another passage in divine Scripture teach us, for truly the Egyptians were drowned in the Red Sea, but the Hebrew people passed through; Moses crossed, but Pharaoh was cast down because weighty sins drowned him, in the way the sacrilegious will be thrown headlong into the lake of burning fire, etc." See also the same thing in serm. 20 on Psalm 118.

St. Augustine (lib. 21 *de Civitate Dei*, cap. 16) speaking about the death of baptized infants: "Not only do they not undergo eternal punishment, but neither do they suffer any purgatorial torments after death." And in ch. 24, speaking about adult faithful who died while they still had light sins, he says: "It is certain that such men, having been purged before the day of judgment by the temporal punishments which their spirits suffer, will not be handed over to torments of eternal fire." He says the same thing in hom. 16 from the book of 50 homilies: "Those who lived in a manner worthy of temporal punishments will pass through a certain purgatorial fire, about which the Apostle speaks when he says they will be saved, yet as if by fire." And in book 2 *de Genes.* against the Manicheans, chap. 20, he says: "He who perhaps did not cultivate his field, and permitted it to be oppressed with thorns, has in this life the curse of his land in all his works, and after this life he will have either the fire of purgation, or eternal punishment." Lastly in Psalm 37, he says: "Because it is said he will be saved, that fire will be avoided, so plainly although he will be saved by fire, still that fire will be graver than any fire a man can suffer in this life." (see above, ch. 6).

This is why when Augustine says (lib. 21 *de Civitate Dei*, cap. 26, Enchirid. Cap. 69) there can be hesitation and questioning as to whether after this life souls are tortured in purgatorial fire, he does not doubt the fact of the punishment of souls, but about the mode and quality; for in the former passage he only doubts whether the purgatorial fire is the same in substance with the fire of hell, of which Matthew 25 says: "Go into the eternal fire." And in the latter he doubts whether after this life souls will burn with that fire of sorrow over the loss of temporal things, with which they usually burn here, when they are very much compelled to lack delightful things.

St. Jerome, at the end of his commentary on Isaiah, says: "As we believe in the eternal torments of the devil and of all the unbelievers and impious who have said in their heart 'there is no god', so we believe that for sinful and impious Christians, whose works must be proved in the fire and also purged, the sentence of the judge will be moderated and mixed with clemency."

St. Gregory says in the *Dialogue* (l. 4 c. 39) "It must be believed that the purgatorial fire is for certain light sins before judgment." And on the third penitential Psalm he says: "I know that after the departure from this life some men will be purged by purgatorial flames, while others will undergo the judgment of eternal damnation."

Origen (homil. 6 in Exodum) says: "He who is saved is saved by fire, so that if perhaps one were to have mixed in some species of lead, the fire shall cook it out and purify it so that all may be made pure gold."

Gregory Nazianzen, in an oration on the Theophany (39), says: "Let these men then if they will, follow our way, which is Christ's way; but if they will not, let them go their own. Perhaps in it they will be baptized with Fire, in that last Baptism which is not only more painful but also longer, which devours wood like grass, and consumes the stubble of every evil."

Basil the Great (*in Isaiah*, ch. 9) "If therefore we have disclosed our sins by confession, we have dried up the grass as it was growing, clearly suitable to be consumed and devoured by the purgatorial fire... It does not altogether threaten destruction and extermination, but beckons to purgation, according to the teaching of the Apostle, 'he will be saved as if by fire'."

Eusebius Emissenus (hom. 3 *de Epiphania*) says: "This infernal punishment will remain for those who, having let go of and not kept their Baptism, will perish forever; but these who lived in a manner worthy of temporal punishments, will pass through the fiery river, through the fearsome ford with fireballs."

Theodoret in his commentary of the Greek of 1 Corinthians 3:15, says: "We believe in this very purgatorial fire, in which the souls of the dead are proven and cleansed, just as gold in a casting furnace." Oecumenius

Ch. X: Purgatory proven from the Fathers 93

says on the same passage: "He will be saved but not before suffering, as is proper for him who passes through fire, and atones for certain lighter sins." Cyprian in lib. 4, epist. 2 says: "It is one thing for sins to be cleansed by a long period of suffering, and emended by a long fire, and another for all sins to be cleansed by martyrdom." (see above, p. 23)

Jerome, in book 1 against the Pelagians, says: "But if Origen says that all rational creatures are not to be destroyed, and attributes penance to the devil, what for us who say the devil and his followers, and all the impious and transgressors perish perpetually, and Christians, if they have been forestalled by sin, are going to be saved after penalties?

Paulinus (epist. 1 ad Amandum), says: "On account of this we eagerly ask that, as a brother of prayer you might unite your labors to ours, that the merciful God would grant rest to his soul by the drops of his mercy through your prayers, etc." Boethius (lib. 4 *Prosa* 4), "Do you bequeath no prayers for souls after the death of the body? And indeed, I think some suffer bitter punitive punishments, others purgatorial clemency." St. Isidore (lib. 1 *de divinis officiis*, c. 18), "For when the Lord says, 'Whoever sins against the Holy Spirit, it will not be remitted to him either in this life or in the next,' he shows that there are certain sins which will be forgiven, and will be cleansed in a certain purgatorial fire."

St. Bede, commenting on Psalm 37, says: "Certain men commit some graver and lighter venial sins, and therefore it is necessary that such men as these be rebuked in wrath, that is, be placed in the purgatorial fire in the meantime before the day of judgment, so that the things which are unclean in them might be burned by it, and so at length they will be suited to be among those to be crowned at God's right hand." In the same place he says that this fire is graver than the punishments of thieves, of martyrs, etc.

St. Peter Damien (*in serm. 2 de S. Andræa*), "Do not flatter yourself if a lighter penance is assigned for a more serious sin due to mildness or dissimulation, since whatever you do not do here must be completed in the purgatorial fires, because the Most High seeks fruits worthy of repentance."

St. Anselm on 1 Corinthians 3:15 says: "For the purgatorial fire must be believed to be before the resurrection of bodies for certain lesser faults."

St. Bernard (*serm. de obitu Humberti*), says: "Time flies irrevocably, brethren, and while you think you are avoiding this minimal punishment, you incur a fuller one, for know this, that after this life whatever was neglected here will be repaid a hundred-fold in purgatory, even to the last farthing. I know how hard it is for a man of dissolute life to take up discipline, for a talkative man to endure silence, for a man accustomed to wandering to remain in one place, but it will be harder and much harder to bear the discomforts to come."

Lactantius (lib. 7 cap. 21), said: "Whose sins are greater by weight or number, will be bound in the fire and burned, etc."

Hilary on Psalm 118, on the words: *My soul desired and longed for the judgments of thy justice,* says: "We will face that indefatigable fire, in which those grave punishments will be suffered by the soul to be cleansed of its sins.

CHAPTER XI
The Same is Asserted from Reason

HE *fourth* argument is taken from reason.

1) *The first reason*: Certain sins are venial, and only worthy of temporal punishment. But it can happen that when a man dies with only these sorts of sins, it is necessary for them to be purged in the next life.

Moreover, that certain sins are venial is proven from James 1, "Each and everyone is held by his concupiscence, when concupiscence begins it prepares sin, when the sin has been consummated, it begets death." Here he describes venial sin from the imperfection of the act. Nor does the distinction of the heretics on imputation have place here, for James explains the process of sin *secundum se*, and he teaches after the temptation of concupiscence, which can be present without being carried out, that sin immediately follows if someone is not careful; for from concupiscence delectation arises in the lower part, which is some sin, but still not deadly, if deliberate consent of the mind is not present, therefore he adds: "But if the sin will have been consummated," namely, adding clear consent, "it begets death."

Besides, 1 Corinthians 3:15 says: "He that builds with wood, grass and straw will be saved as if by fire." Here venial sin is described from the levity of matter, and seeing that we understand the words of the Apostle to be either on this life or on the next, either on doctrine or on all works, he necessary is compelled to explain by wood, grass and straw, venial sins, seeing that one who so has them, is saved, as if by fire.

St. Augustine, lib. 83, quaest. 26, says: "Some are sins of weakness, some of inexperience, some of malice; weakness is contrary to strength; inexperience to wisdom; malice to goodness; thus, whoever knows what is strong, the wisdom of God, can judge what are venial sins, and whoever knows what is the goodness of God, can judge that a certain penalty is due for some sins, both here and in the coming age, which has been treated enough, it can be judged with probability who will not be compelled to fruitful and lamentable penance, although they professed sins and for whom there is altogether no hope of salvation, except they will offer sacrifice to God, with a contrite spirit by penance."

Lastly, from reason: for it is not understandable how an idle word by its nature would be worthy of God's perpetual hatred and eternal flames, for this man would be held for the stupidest man in the world, who, on account of the lightest offense of a friend, that was not done in a bad spirit, would refuse to be his friend any longer, nay more, to even pursue him unto death, who had just a while earlier been his friend. Therefore, it remains that there are certain venial sins that are worthy of merely temporal punishment. Moreover, the fact that some men die with venial sins, and hence they need temporal purgation in another life is proven in this way. Someone can, while he dies, have a will to remain in venial sin, therefore such a sin cannot be blotted out in death. Furthermore, "the just man falls seven times a day" (Proverbs 24:16), and many die immediately, so how credible is it that some men do not die with venial sin? This is the first reason.

Ch. XI: Purgatory is proven from reason

2) *The second* reason: When sinners are reconciled to God, the whole temporal punishment is not always forgiven, but it can happen and often does, that in someone's whole life he will not make satisfaction fully for those temporal punishments: therefore, necessarily he ought to be put in Purgatory. The major proposition is briefly proven since it is expressly shown in other places: 2 Kings 12:13, when David said: "I have sinned against the Lord," and the prophet said, "The Lord has also taken away your sin, you will not die. Just the same, because you have caused the enemies of the Lord to blaspheme on account of this word, the son that was born to you will die." Numbers 12:10, when Miriam murmured against the Lord, she was punished with the plague of leprosy, by when Moses prayed for her, her sin was forgiven and still God wanted to punish her so that she would suffer punishment for one week.

Calvin responds to these and similar things (*Institutes* lib. 3 cap. 4 § 31), that there are two types of scourges of God: certain ones are properly for punishments and inflicted by God as a judge, in vengeance for sins committed to satisfy justice; and certain ones that are castigations that are inflicted by God, as father, not in vengeance for sins committed but as a remedy for the future; without a doubt as a man is admonished by a whip, lest he would again sin so easily. Calvin says the first kind pertains to enemies alone, the second only to friends, and hence, when these punishments are suffered not for justice, it is not necessary that their debt would remain after death, when there is no danger of falling back into sin.

But Calvin labors in vain. Even if one affirmed the whip of the just is really paternal castigations and remedies against future sins, still it must be acknowledged as a true punishment, and satisfaction is due for a past fault *from justice*. For, in 2 Kings 12:14, the reason why David is punished is clearly expressed, and it is not said: Do not sin again, but "Because you have caused the enemies of God to blaspheme."

Next, death is the true punishment for original sin, and just men suffer the punishment not to abstain from sin but to satisfy divine justice, which is clear because it is not inflicted by God after sin, like paternal castigations, rather it is established in law before our sin just like a punishment for sin, and the same perseveres after sin and even the remission of sin, which we see in Genesis 2:17, "On whatever day you shall eat, you will die," and Romans 5:12, "Through one man sin entered into this word, and through sin death, etc., in which all have sinned." And Romans 6:23, "The wages of sin are death." And Calvin himself in the *Institutes* (lib. 2, c. 1 §8) clearly confesses that death is a true punishment for sin. *Lastly*, how can death be a paternal scourging to establish fear of sin? For one that dies can no longer be corrected.

Apart from this common death, which is the penalty of original sin, we have other examples in the Scripture of those who were punished with a violent death although they were forgiven for sin. Nevertheless, there are many examples showing that death cannot be a paternal castigation in remedy of a future sin. Exodus 32:14, where God spared the people at Moses' prayer, and still Moses ordered many thousands of the people to be killed in vengeance for sin without any crime; likewise in Numbers

14:45 when the people murmured and God was pleased by Moses, still a great many perished in the desert. Moreover, it is unbelievable that from so many thousands there was not even one that did penance for the crime. 3 Kings 13:24, the Prophet of the Lord, because he disobeyed the voice of the Lord, was snuffed out by a lion, according to what had been foretold to him by another prophet, and still that we should understand that his sin was remitted, and that he died in a holy death, the lion touched neither his body nor the beast of burden that carried him, but instead guarded them both until men came to bury him. *Lastly,* 1 Corinthians 11:30 where it says: "There are many fools among you, and many sleep." There, Ambrose and others explain that the Apostle indicates that in the primitive Church there were many that took communion unworthily and were punished by God with death, still that this sin was first remitted is clear from the very thing the Apostle adds in verse 32: "We are rebuked by the Lord lest we might be condemned with the world."

Let two famous testimonies of St. Augustine be added to this. *The first* is *in Joann.* tract. 124: "A man is compelled to endure [trial] even after his sins have been forgiven, although the first sin was the reason why he came into the first misery. The penalty is more protracted than the fault, so that the fault would not be considered small were the penalty to end with itself. This is also why it is, either for the demonstration of our debt of misery, or for the amendment of our passing life, or for the exercise of the necessary patience, that man is kept through time in the penalty, even when he is no longer held by his sin as liable to everlasting damnation." The *second* is his commentary on Psalm 50 (51), where he says: "*You have loved truth*", this is, the unpunished sins of those whom you forgive you have not yet dismissed, so you have preferred mercy to also save the truth, you forgave the one confessing, you forgave, but he underwent punishment, so that mercy and truth would be preserved."

The assumption of this argument is proved because many who committed a very great number of sins are converted at the point of death when they cannot do penance. This is why certainly it follows that after this life they must make satisfaction. They answer that in death all things are blotted out. *On the other hand*: Death is a penalty for original sin, and therefore common to all, even infants, so other punishments ought to be found for actual sins. Besides, God would act unjustly if it did not seem that he had providence for our affairs, if with one and the same penalty, *i.e.* natural death, he were to punish great sins as well as small, many and few.

3) *The third* reason is taken from the common opinion of all nations, *i.e.* the Jews, Mahometans, pagans, and among them both philosophers and poets confess it. From the Jews, it is clear from 2 Maccabees, 12:42, for, at least the trust which is placed in Livy must be placed in that book. Besides, Josephus, the son of Gorion, in his book *On the Jewish War*, c. 19, he indicates that the Jews customarily prayed for the dead, but not for those who killed themselves.

From the Mahometans, it is clear from the Qur'an, where they precisely confess a purgatory. From the pagans it is clear from Plato in the Gorgias, and Phaedo from Cicero in *Scipio's dream*, and Virgil (*Aeneid* lib. 6):

Ch. XI: Purgatory is proven from reason

For this, the chastisement of evils past
Is suffered here, and full requital paid.[7]

And from Claudianus, book 2, *in Ruffinum* near the end:

For thrice a thousand years he had forced these through countless shapes,
he sends them back purged by Lethæus' stream.[8]

Nor would someone say this argument is especially erroneous and fabulous, seeing that the Pagans and Mahometans think it; those matters upon which nearly all nations agree can hardly otherwise come about except from the natural light common to all men. Those things which are devised and created by men are manifold and different for the difference of every nation. So, just as God exists, on which point all nations agree, we say it is most true, but we do not, nevertheless, receive different gods in particular, many of which each nation makes for itself, and just as after this life there are punishments and rewards, on which all agree, we receive as true but do not receive the different fables in which they explain this (that there are punishments and rewards after this life, the knowledge of divine providence teaches all men, but the fables they make by themselves), so also the confession of purgatory,

---

[7] Ergo exercentur poenis veterumque malorum
supplicia expendunt. –Aeneid, l. 6.739-40.

[8] *Quos ubi per varios amnes, per mille figuras*
Egit Lethæo purgatos flumine, etc.
Translator's note: *Lethæus* refers, at least in its use in Ovid, to a river in Hades where the dead would drink and forget.

in which nearly all nations agree, we must say is a confession of the light of reason; for knowledge of the same providence taught Purgatory that also taught hell and paradise, at least in a general and somewhat confused manner, because without a doubt we see punishments and rewards so distributed in this life that the wicked have many goods and the good many evils, as many as you like, thence we judge the divine providence distributed justice in another life, as well as the true distribution of rewards and penalties.

Again we see from these those who depart from this life that some are very good, others very evil, and others somewhat good and somewhat bad; this is why we judge by the natural light that there is, after this life, eternal punishments for the very wicked, eternal rewards for the very good and temporary punishments and by these the passage to the rewards for those who are somewhat evil or good. Plato and others followed this reasoning, who confessed purgatory provided only with the light of natural reason.

4) *The fourth* reason is taken from apparitions of souls that declared they were in purgatory, and also implored assistance from the living; seeing that very serious men relate these apparitions, we do not unduly consider them true, although Luther and the Centuriators mock them. St. Gregory (*Dialog.* lib, 4, cap. 40) writes about the soul of Paschasius, who appeared in the baths of Puteoli to St. the Bishop St. Germane, and he was freed by the latter's prayers. And ch. 55, he writes another similar example. Besides, in regard to a certain monk for whom Gregory himself offered 30 Masses that he had commanded said, he later learned that he was liberated by that apparition.

Ch. XI: Purgatory is proven from reason

Gregory of Turin, in his book *de gloria confess.*, ch. 5, writes that a certain holy Virgin by the name of Vitalina that had just died showed herself to St. Martin and that she abided in purgatory on account of a certain light sin, and a little later she was freed by the prayers of the same St. Martin.

St. Peter Damian, in an epistle to Desiderius, writes that Blessed Severinus, the Bishop of Cologne, appeared to a certain priest of the same Church, and showed to him that he was still severely tormented in purgatory because he did not say the canonical hours at distinct times, but piled up all the hours together in the morning, so that he could be more freely employed in Imperial business for the whole day.

St. Bede (lib. 3 hist. Anglorum, ch. 19) writes about St. Fursæus who rose from the dead to tell many things which he saw in regard to the punishments of purgatory, and in book 5, ch. 13, he relates a marvelous vision of a certain Diethelm, who similarly was dead and later came back to life by a miracle and related about hell, purgatory and paradise, and his life following, as well as the spiritual fruit which is worked in many other places, and Bede witnesses that this was a true vision.

St. Bernard, in the life of St. Malachi, relates that St. Malachi's dead sister did not appear to him once, although she still abided in purgatorial punishments, and at length, after frequent offering of the Eucharist to God, she was liberated; and in book 1 of the life of St. Bernard (ch. 10) William Abbas, who wrote the life of Bernard, relates that while he was still living a monk that had died appeared to Bernard, laboring in purgatory and a little later he was freed by the prayers and sacrifices of the holy man. The author of this life wrote that St. Bernard himself usually related this vision.

In the first book of the life of St. Anselm we likewise read that St. Anselm consumed a whole year with daily sacrifices, and at length a dead friend appeared to him, for whom he had prayed so long, and learned that he was liberated from Purgatory. Many similar things can be read with Vincentium, lib. 23, *Speculi historialis*, in the revelations of St. Bridgett and in the life of the extraordinary St. Christina; what we have advanced here, however, is more authentic.

The Centuriators respond that these are fables. But it is not believable that so many holy men would have wanted to deceive, nor even to have been deceived themselves, seeing that they had the spirit of discretion and were friends of God.

Lastly, it stands to reason that because the opinion which abolishes purgatory is not only false, but even pernicious; accordingly, it makes men sluggish in avoiding sins and doing good works. For one that thinks there is no purgatory, but that all sins are abolished by death for those who die with faith, will easily say to himself: To what end do I labor in fasting, prayers, continence, almsgiving? Why do I cheat my heart of delights and pleasures? Seeing that in death I will have a few or many sins they will all be blotted out. But someone that thinks that apart from hell, the most bitter fire of Purgatory remains and whatever was not blotted out here by due works of penance are going to be washed away there, certainly he will go out more diligent and cautious.

CHAPTER XII
Arguments from the Scriptures are Answered

T remains to answer the arguments of our adversaries, which are taken partly from partly from Scripture, the partly from the Fathers and from natural reason.

1) *The first* objection is from Psalm 126 (127):4, "When he gave a dream to his beloved, behold the inheritance of the Lord"; therefore, there is no Purgatory between the death of the faithful and the attainment of the heavenly inheritance.

I respond: The Psalm treats on the general resurrection, as St. Augustine rightly explains, and this is the sense of the words: When he gave a dream to his beloved, that is, when all the elect sleep by corporal death, behold the Lord's inheritance, *i.e.* then the inheritance of Christ, will immediately appear to those rising in glory with all his elect. That inheritance is also the wages of the same Christ, who acquired us by his passion and death. Therefore, the inheritance and the wages of the son are the same thing, as well as the fruit of the womb; for sons of God by adoption are the Lord's inheritance and the same sons who are called the fruit of the womb, are the wages of the same Lord.

Add, that in the Hebrew text which our adversaries prefer to the Latin, it does not say, "when he gave," but "he will so give," וְתִי וּב [*chen itthen*]. Hence, the whole of the argument comes to ruin, for when the inheritance of the Lord will come is what is explained.

2) *The second* objection is from Ecclesiast. 9:10, "Whatever your hand can do, do it with urgency, because neither work, nor reason, nor wisdom, nor knowledge will be in hell, where you are rushing headlong." For it seems the wise man means with these words that there is no remedy in the next life.

Some respond that these are said by Solomon in the person of the impious, who not only remove Purgatory, but even hell and believe in nothing apart from this life. Others teach that Solomon spoke to those who live idly and shamefully, and are on the road to hell: in such a passage it is most true that there is no remedy or solace. St. Jerome touches upon each exposition in his commentary. But St. Gregory (*Dialog.* lib. 4, c. 39 accommodates all these things suitably enough to those also which are deduced to Purgatory; for only those can be purged and assisted by the prayers of the living, who, while they lived here on earth, merited it by their good works so that they could be assisted in the next life. This is why everyone ought to do whatever good they can in this life, because in the next they will not be helped except for those things which those alive here can merit for their assistance.

3) *The third* objection is from Ecclesiastes 11:3, "If a tree will fall to the south, or to the north, in whatever place it fell, there it will lie." Thence, a third place is not given, namely Purgatory, from where one may go out at some time.

I respond: Wisdom literally speaks on *corporal death*, and means to say, so men necessarily are going to die and when they are dead, *per se* they are never going to rise, just as a tree when it falls, stays there and will rot where it fell. Nevertheless, if we wish to accommodate these things to

Ch. XII: Objections from Scripture are refuted

the state of the soul, the men who pertain to Purgatory fell to the south, *i.e.* to the state of eternal salvation and in that state will remain saved forever; or certainly it could be said for "the south" heavenly glory, but through the north Gehenna is understood, but not all fall to the south or north. Moreover, this passage impedes no assertion of Purgatory, because it can also be understood that if it would impede the assertion of Purgatory, it would also impede an assertion of that place to which the Fathers descended before Christ came there, whether that place, the bosom of Abraham, or the limbo of the Fathers, remained perpetually in that place. See Jerome in his commentary, and Bernard, sermon 49 *ex parvis*.

4) *The fourth objection* is from Ezechiel 18:21-22, "If the impious will do penance for all his sins, which he committed ... I will not remember his iniquities." But how, Peter Martry says, shall God not remember the iniquity of his friends if he punishes them so severely in purgatory?

I respond in two ways. *Firstly*, to not remember iniquity is nothing other than to not preserve enmity with someone that sinned; for if to remember iniquity were to punish wicked merits, to remember justice would be to reward good merits. But our adversaries do not concede that to reward justice is to remunerate good merits, lest it would seem they are compelled to admit the merits of the just, so they ought also not concede that to remember iniquity is to punish iniquities, for Ezechiel speaks on justice and iniquity in the same way.

Secondly, it can be answered that to remember iniquity is indeed to punish, but to punish *forever*; for when we read the same thing in verse 24: "If the just man turns away from justice, no one will remember his justice." We are compelled to so explain that justices are said to be handed over to oblivion, not because they would have been paid back with some temporal reward, but they will not free a man from hell, nor will they be remunerated with the eternal reward; for otherwise, the good works of the impious are not cheated of temporal reward, as the Fathers teach (Chrysostom, homil. 67 ad populum Antiochenum; Jerome, *in cap. 29 Ezechiel*; Augustine, *de Civitate Dei*, lib. 5, cap. 15; Gregory, *Homil.* 40 in Evangelia), and it is gathered from the very words of Luke 16:25, "You have received good things in your life."

5) *The fifth* objection is from Matthew 25, where we discover only two classes of men: "Come ye blessed," (v. 34) and: "Depart ye cursed" (v. 41). Likewise, in the last chapter of Mark, verse 16: "He who believes and will be baptized will be saved, but he that does not believe will be condemned." Then in John 3:18, "He who believes shall not be judged, he that does not believe, has already been judged." "Therefore," Brenz says, "no place remains for purgatory, although there are only two places after this life."

I respond: In the last judgment, which is argued in Mathew 25, there rightly are only two classes because then Purgatory will end, and thereafter only two places remain, Paradise and hell. Moreover, he who believes will be saved and is not judged, *i.e.* he is not condemned, provided he also adds the other things which are required, for faith of itself justifies and saves, if there is no other impediment. Just as we usually say the tree is born from this seed, or if the heat of the sun does not cease, the humor of the waters, and if some other things are required, but not right away, the one who will be saved by faith will be saved without Purgatory, for many are saved, still thus as if by fire, as we proved above from the words of the Apostle.

6) *The sixth* objection is from Luke 23:43; Christ tells the thief that converted in the last hour: "Today you will be with me in paradise." Therefore, Peter Martyr and Bernadine Ochinus say that purgatory does not remain for those who do not do penance in this life. *I respond:* that very hard death born with a patient spirit, and so admirable a confession at a time when the Apostles themselves denied Christ, could justly be accounted to have made full satisfaction. Add, that the privileges of a few do not make law.

7) *The seventh* objection is from Romans 8:1, "There is no damnation for those who are in Christ Jesus."

I respond: Paul, in that place, does not argue about concupiscence, and means to say: those who are in Christ Jesus, and fortified by his grace do not consent to the motions of their flesh. Therefore, this passage is not opposed to purgatory, rather the heresy of our adversaries, who would have it those movements are also true sins, even when the just man does not consent to them.

8) *The eighth* objection is from 2 Corinthians 5:1, "We know if our earthly house of this habitation were destroyed that we have a building of God, a house not made by hand, but eternal in heaven." Consequently, after death pious men pass into heaven without purgatory.

I respond: St. Paul only asserts that the heavenly home is open after death, not that it is open before death; but he does not say that all pious men make the passage to heaven immediately after death, but shows the contrary when he says in verse 3: "Nevertheless, that we be found clothed, not naked." For by these words he means they are clothed by those merits and virtues and hence they did perfect penance in this life, right away they are led into their heavenly home; but others are saved, yet, as if by fire, as he himself says in 1 Corinthians 3:15.

9) *The ninth* objection is from 2 Corinthians 5:10, "For we must all be made manifest before the tribunal of Christ so that each and every one may receive what is proper to the body, insofar as he has done, whether good or evil." But if after this life sins are remitted and there was a place for purgation, certainly each and every man would not receive according to what he did in body.

I respond: The teaching of St. Paul is most true, for even those that find the place for remission and purgation in the next life receive nothing, except what they did in body; for they merit that they persevered in faith and charity even to death, so that even after death they can be cleansed and assisted. By that reasoning even holy men after death, even if they properly merited nothing, still might beg from the Lord whatever they want, because they merited it in this life by right living, so that even after this life hey are heard by the Lord. You can see the very thing that we teach in Dionysius, in his book *de Ecclesiastica hierarchia,* last chapter part 3, with St. Augustine (*Enchir.* c. 110 and *de cura pro mortuis,* cap. 1), and with Gregory (*Dialog.* lib. 4, cap. 39). And these things must be understood according to the same mode: "Let him render to each according to his works," (Romans 2:6), and "Bear each other's burden" (Galatians 6:5), and "As a man has sown, so shall he reap" (*ibid.*, 8).

10) *The tenth* objection is from Apocalypse 14:13, "The blessed dead, who died in the Lord, from this time forward the Spirit already says that they should rest from their

Ch. XII: Objections from Scripture are refuted

labors, for their works follow them." But all the pious die in the Lord; so all the pious after death rest, and none suffer in Purgatory.

I respond with St. Anselm, in his commentary on this passage, that "from this time forward" (*amodo*), does not mean each man from death, but from the last judgment, on which St. John speaks throughout the chapter. Therefore, this will be the sense: The blessed dead, who died in the Lord, from this point forward, *i.e.* from the end of this judgment, on which we are speaking now, they will rest from their labors forever; or if that is not proof enough for someone, we can respond with Richard of St. Victor and Haymo on this passage, that St. John speaks about perfect men, and especially on the holy martyrs (those he means to console in this passage), who simply die in the Lord and do not bring anything with them to be purified; for anyone who dies with venial sins, or with punishment due for some temporal thing, they do not simply die in the Lord, but partly in the Lord, by reason of charity, which they carry with themselves, and partly not in the Lord, by reason of the sins which, just the same, they bring with them. Nor will it seem a marvel that we say some men die partly in the Lord and partly not in the Lord if we read St. Augustine (*Contra duas epistolas Pelagianorum*, lib. 3 cap. 3) where he says the same men in this life are partly sons of God and partly sons of this world. And that is enough from the Scriptures.

CHAPTER XIII
Objections from the Fathers are Answered

RENZ advances objections from the Fathers.
1) *Firstly* from Cyprian, who in the first treatise against Demetrianum, says in the end: "When they will have left here, now there is no place for penance, no effect of satisfaction."

I respond: He speaks on the satisfaction for sin which precedes justification, for the Fathers precisely place a twofold satisfaction. One before justification, whereby God is pleased from what is fitting and inclined to grant remission for sin. Daniel speaks about this (4:24), "Redeem your sins with almsgiving." The other is after justification, whereby he condignly satisfies God for punishment. Here Cyprian speaks on the first kind, which is clear from the preceding words, in which he says: "We exhort you, to make satisfaction to God while still some time remains in this world and emerge from the depths of the darkness of superstition to the pure light of true religion." Likewise, from the following words: for after what Brenz cites, it immediately follows: "This life is either lost, or held."

2) *Secondly*, he advances Chrysostom (hom. 2 *de Lazaro*), who says: "When we will have departed from this life, it is no longer for us to do penance, nor to wash away what we have committed... For those men that do not wash away sins in the present life, they will later find some consolation."

I respond: He speaks on the remission of mortal sins, for example, of the rich man, who is tortured in hell, he warns us not to delay conversion for another life. But no Catholic teaches that mortal sins are remitted in Purgatory.

3) *Thirdly*, they advance Ambrose (*de bono mortis*, ch. 2), and he says: "Whoever does not receive the remission of sins in this life, he will not there, namely in the country of the blessed."

I respond: Ambrose speaks about the remission of mortal sins, for he adds, explaining: "But he will not, because he cannot come to eternal life since eternal life is the remission of sins." He calls eternal life the grace of justification, which is a certain life beginning with eternity; unless we begin eternal life here we will never come to the glory of the blessed.

4) *Fourthly*, Peter Martyr objects with the same St. Ambrose, who, in chapter 23 of Luke, as well as sermon 46 says: "I read the tears of Peter, but not satisfaction."

I respond: In that passage satisfaction is called excuse. For we usually say in our common speech: I will satisfy him, that is, I will cleanse the criminal charge with words and I shall show that I was unjustly accused; consequently, in that passage Ambrose praises Peter because he did not excuse his sin in the way that Adam did, but instead confessed it with tears and accused himself. For he so adds: "Peter rightly wept and was silent, because what is usually wept over is not usually excused, and what cannot be defended, can be washed away... I find that he wept, I do not find what he said, because without a doubt Peter said nothing in purgation of himself."

5) *Fifthly*, Calvin objects using Augustine who says, in tract. 49 *in Joannem*, "All souls have, when they depart this life, their different receptions, they have the joy of good and the torments of evil, but when the resurrection

happens, the joy of the good will be increased and the torments of the wicked will be more grave, seeing that they will be tortured with their body... The rest, which is given immediately after death, if he is worthy of it, then each one receives it when he dies."

I respond: Death brings joy and rest right away to all who die in charity, for in death all become certain of their eternal salvation, because it advances a great joy, but in different ways for the diversity of merits; for it is given to certain men without a mixture of suffering, for some, not without a mixture of temporal punishment; as St. Augustine often teaches the same thing.

6) *Sixthly,* they object the book *Hypognostici* of Augustine: "The faith of Catholics believes with divine authority that the first place is the kingdom of heaven, the second, hell, where all apostates or those foreign to the faith of Christ will experience eternal tortures; the third place we are altogether ignorant of, nay more, we also do not find it in the Scriptures. The same has Sermon 14, *de verbis Apostoli,* and lib. 1 c. 28 of *Peccatorum Meritis et remissione.*

I respond: He speaks about eternal places, for he writes against Pelagius, who found a third place for children that were not baptized, whom he would have it were blessed with a certain natural beatitude outside of hell and outside of the kingdom of heaven. But Augustine, or whoever was the author of *Hypognostici,* did not deny a third temporary place after this life; it can be understood from the fact that the Catholic faith teaches that apart from heaven and hell, there was before the passion of Christ the bosom of Abraham, where souls of the holy Fathers abided. Thus, Erasmus ineptly placed in the margin next to those words:

Ch. XIII: Objections from the Fathers are answered 115

"The third we altogether do not know is purgatory", in other words, Purgatory would be this third place which the Catholic faith does not know.

7) *Seventhly*, Peter Martyr objects using the same Augustine, explaining that of Psalm 31 (32) *Blessed are they, whose sins have been covered*, says: "If he [God] covered sins, he refused to notice them; if he refused to notice, he refused to punish; he refused to acknowledge but, preferred to forgive."

I respond: He speaks on *eternal* punishment, for on the temporal punishment which God requires, it is clear from the citations we made of Augustine above in tract. 124 *in Joann.* and on *Psalm 50.*

8) *Eighthly*, they advance Augustine from epistle 54 to Macedonius, where he says that after this life there will be no correction of morals.

I respond: This has no bearing on the matter at hand, for even if there were not, after this life, a place where the dissolute convert and correct their morals. Nevertheless, there will be a place where the light sins of the just (which cannot be called outrages), will be purged as well as temporal punishment suffered for crimes that were already forgiven.

9) *Ninthly*, they object again using Augustine from epistle 80 to Hesychius, where he says: "In whatever place someone will have found his last day, the last day of the world will seize him in this state, because in whatever state he was in on the day he died, so he will be judged in that state on that day."

I respond: Augustine means after this life merits or demerits will not increase, and thus, everyone that is going to be judged for glory, or for hell, and to greater or lesser rewards or torments, will be judged exactly by the works he had done before his death.

10) *Tenthly,* they object from Theophylactus, who on chapter 8 of Matthew says: "After the soul has gone out it does not wander into the world; for the souls of the just are in the hand of God, but the souls of sinners are lead hence, like the soul of the rich man."

I respond: Theophylactus indicates that souls do not wander freely about the world, as demons do, but are closed in their shelters, and although he does not call to mind any besides those two places, nevertheless, he does not exclude another. Moreover, we can recall the souls which are lead to Purgatory, to whichever of those two places which he posits; for because they are just, they can rightly be said to be in the hand of God, although not in the kingdom of heaven, and similarly, they can be said to be in hell because Purgatory is part of hell, or certainly a neighboring area.

11) *In the eleventh place,* they object with St. Jerome, who says on c. 9 of Amos: "When a soul is released from the corporeal bonds from which it wills to fly, or from which it is compelled to go, it has freedom, or it is led to hell, on which it has been written, 'Who will confess you in hell?' or certainly it will be lifted up to heaven."

I respond: Jerome does not speak on natural death, but on the freeing of the soul from the body by a speculation, for he disputes in that place on the impious soul, which, whenever it will turn itself in thought, there it will find God as an avenger. Therefore, when he said: "Or will certainly be lifted to heaven," he adds, "Where there are spiritual things of wickedness in heaven, even if they mean to claim for themselves knowledge of circumcision, and

Ch. XIII: Objections from the Fathers are answered

having been conceived in humility, dwell in the mountains, and there it will be of no avail to avoid the probing hand of God, or try to avoid the eyes of the Lord, and to arrive in the last confines of salty waves, even if there the Lord will deliver to the torturous and ancient serpent, who is the enemy and avenger and he will bite the soul. Also, taken with vices and sins it will be struck by the sword of the Lord, that through tortures and punishments they be returned to the Lord."

CHAPTER XIV
Answer to Objections Raised from Reason

LASTLY, they take up arguments from reason.
1) *The first* reason, is that after sin has been remitted no punishment remains, for remission of sin takes place by the merit of the Passion of Christ, which is infinite and sufficient to take away every sin and punishment, therefore nothing remains to be purged after justification.

I respond: First by turning the argument on its head, for if Christ satisfies for all of our sin and punishment, why do we still suffer so many things after our sins have been remitted, and at length also die? Should they say that they are paternal castigations to remedy future sin, we can ask why do infants get sick, who do not have the capacity for actual sin? Therefore, I say the merit of Christ suffices to take away all sin and punishment, but it must be applied to be efficacious, otherwise all men would be saved.

Furthermore, the application happens through our acts and the Sacraments. God willed that after Baptism the merit of Christ would be applied with contrition, and confession with the absolution of the priest to abolish sin, and further, be applied by satisfying works to take away temporal punishment, for eternal punishment is commuted to temporal when sin is remitted. This is because, when sin is remitted friendship is restored, and consequently the right to glory is given, and hence, he ought not be punished forever because in that mode, the soul would never attain to eternal glory and yet justice be exacted, since sin should be punished in some mode, thus eternal punishment is changed into temporal punishment. Something about the reason for it was said above, and more will be said in the disputation on satisfaction.

2) *The second* reason: In Baptism all sin and punishment is remitted, but Penance is a certain remembrance of Baptism, or rather, it is a certain type of Baptism; therefore, nothing remains to be cleansed after penance.

I respond: If the sacrament of Penance were received in an integral and Catholic manner, as embracing contrition, confession and satisfaction, full and now perfect, the whole argument can be admitted; but if it is received in favor of absolution alone, in which the sacrament especially consists, the consequent is denied. For there is a great distinction between the sacrament of ablution and the sacrament of absolution, the ignorance of which is the reason for every error on satisfaction, the keys and indulgences, as well as on Purgatory.

Therefore, we say in the Sacrament of Baptism, God acts very generously, and applies the merit of Christ through that one action of ablution, to take away every sin and punishment of the next life, that is, both of hell and purgatory; but for the temporal punishments of this life, not even Baptism takes away, as is clear in sick and dying children that are baptized. But in the Sacrament of absolution God still holds back his hand, and applies the merit of Christ to take away sin and eternal punishment; nevertheless, it still requires works of penance, in which we make recompense for temporal punishments; this is clear from Hebrews 6, where the Apostle says: "It is impossible for those who are once illumined (*i.e.* the baptized) to again be renewed to penance", namely baptismal penance, because God only once uses that generosity. And in chapter 10 he says: "For if we sin wilfully after having the knowledge of the truth," *i.e.* after the illumination of baptism, "there is now left no sacrifice for sins," *i.e.* another suffering Christ and dying is not left behind, with whom we could again die by Baptism; for so all the Greek and Latin fathers explain these two places.

From that we have a notable argument for Purgatory. For the opposed particle is placed, "the terrible expectation of judgment and the blaze of fire, which is going to consume the adversaries". For if that would only mean the fire of hell, it would follow that all who sin after Baptism are necessarily going to be damned, or certainly that Paul speaks ineptly. Nor would we rightly say another Baptism does not remain for the sinner after Baptism but hell, if apart from Baptism there are other remedies, as there really are.

Therefore we must say that by fire, St. Paul understands fire in general, whether of hell or purgatory, so that this would be the sense: another Baptism does not remain for the sinner after Baptism, nor some equivalent remedy, *i.e.* just as easy which would free him from all fault on the spot; but fire necessary remains, either perpetual, if a man would not convert, or temporal, if he converts; nevertheless this temporal fire of purgatory will be in another life, unless the fire of affliction, taken up voluntarily, will purge a man in this life, and this is what we call satisfaction. The same thing is clear from the Fathers, who on that account call the Baptism of water easy, and compare it to a ship easily passing over the waters, and penitence a laborious baptism of tears, fire and a second plank after the shipwreck. Thereupon, reason persuades the same thing; for after the first reconciliation,

Ch. XIV: Objections from reason are answered

one sins so much more grievously the more ungrateful he is, as well as the greater the knowledge and assistance he possesses. See Gregory Nazianzen in his oration on *Holy Lights*, as well as Theodoret in the *Epitome of the divine decrees*, second to last chapter, as well as John Damascene, lib. 4 c. 10.

3) *The third* reason: The honor of Christ ought to remain spotless, for he alone is our liberator and redeemer. But if we make satisfaction, now we divide honor with Christ, for we become our own redeemers in some part, and we would owe not our whole salvation to Christ, but only part of it.

I respond: If it is a question of words, Scripture clearly says, "Redeem your sins with almsgiving," and Philippians 2:12 says, "Work out your salvation with fear and trembling." There, man is called his own redeemer and savior, but no injury is done to Christ on that account, the whole strength of our works and satisfaction depends upon the blood of Christ, and if we redeem sins, or work out our salvation, we do it by a gift of his spirit to us, or rather the very spirit of Christ works these things in us, just as nothing detracts from God which will be done through secondary causes. Nay more, it is added more to his glory because from that the efficacy of the power of God appears even more, seeing that he could not only do it, but even give to other things the force of operation.

4) *The fourth* reason: If satisfaction were applied to us by the works of Christ, either there would be two satisfactions joined together, one of Christ and the other ours, or only one. If two, then the same fault is punished by these and two punishments correspond to one sin; yet if one, either this is of Christ and then we do not make

satisfaction, or ours and then Christ is excluded, or we truly divide the honor with Christ; for he will pay for the sin, we for the punishment.

I respond: There are three manners of speaking. *The first* is of those who assert that assert it is only one and that is of Christ, and we properly do not make satisfaction but only do something under the watchful eye of God who applies the satisfaction of Christ to us, which is to say our works are not without conditions, without which the satisfaction of Christ would not be applied to us, or in general, they are dispositions; So thinks Michael de Bay (Bajus) in his book *de Indulgentiis,* in the last chapter, which seems to me to be an erroneous opinion, for Scripture and the fathers everywhere call our works satisfactions, and of sinners redemptions. Lastly if a just man can merit eternal life from his works *de condigno,* why can he not satisfy for temporal punishment, which is less?

The second manner of speaking is of others, that there are two but one depends on the other; this mode does not seem improbable to me; for even if one would suffice, still, for the greater glory of God, whom it satisfies, and the greater honor of the man making satisfaction, it pleased Christ to join our woks to his, in the way in which one drop of his blood sufficed to redeem the world, and still he willed to pour forth all his blood that it would be a most copious redemption; in this way even a just adult man has the right by a two-fold title to the same glory, one by the merits of Christ communicated to him by grace, the other from his own merits.

The third manner of speaking seems more probable, that there is only one actual satisfaction, and this is ours. Christ is not excluded, or his satisfaction, because by his satisfaction we have the grace from where we make our satisfaction, and in this mode it is said that the satisfaction of Christ is applied to us; not that it makes immediate satisfaction to take away the temporal punishment due to us, but that it takes it away by a medium, insofar as we have grace from his satisfaction, without which our satisfaction would count for nothing.

Apart from these objections of the heretics we will also strike to other objections which theologians usually propose, to more clearly elucidate the truth of the matter.

5) *The fifth* objection from reason: In Purgatory there is no merit, therefore no satisfaction; for the same thing is required to merit and satisfy, and every satisfaction is meritorious.

I respond: The consequent must be denied, for certain common things are also required for merit and satisfaction, but also certain things of our own, from a defect of which something is merit without satisfaction, and vice versa. *Gratia inhabitans* is required for both, but this does not suffice. For it is required for satisfaction that a work, which is done, must be penitential, which is not required for merit. Freedom is required for merit, which praise follows; that which is not required for satisfaction, since when someone is compelled by a judge to pay a debt, he truly satisfies, even if compelled; on that account state of life is required to merit. For God, as the agonotheta of our games, wills the present life to exist, in turn, souls which abide in Purgatory, because they are the medium from which to the state between wayfarers and the blessed, or the damned, for they are confirmed in good and yet are still held back from the attainment of the supreme good, and so they can make satisfaction, but not merit, although we can do both, the blessed and the damned, neither.

6) *The sixth reason*, Purgatory is constituted partly for the remission of venial sin, and partly to satisfy for punishment, but neither have place after this life; for it is of him to rise again from fault whose it is to fall into sin, but after this life souls cannot commit venial sins.

Besides, all sins are remitted by penance, but after this life there is no penance, for death is the same for man as the fall for the angels, as Damascene says (lib. 2 cap. 4). But angels through their fall became immovably fixed in evil. Next, in this life, as a just man can merit an increase of grace, so also remission of venial offenses. But after this life, there is no merit. Further, on punishment it is so proven: Punishment is on account of sin, and as sin increases, so also punishment, as sin decreases, so also the punishment, therefore, without sin, punishment is removed.

I respond: There are not lacking those who, on account of these arguments, deny that venial sin can be remitted after this life, as St. Thomas relates in his Commentary on the Sentences, (4 dist. 21 q. 1 art. 2). But they were saying all venial sins are remitted in death itself through the final grace. But they erred because Scripture and the Fathers clearly teach that after this life, light sins are remitted, nor is their foundation solid, for the final grace cannot remit sin which pleases in act, nay more, that which does not displease in some mode. But someone can die in the complacency of venial sin, or certainly without any act such as if he died straight away, or in madness, or sleeping.

Others, such as Scotus (4 dist. 21 quaest. 1) say that sin remains only in man after his acts pass, he is remanded to

Ch. XIV: Objections from reason are answered

punishment and therefore venial sin is said to be remitted in Purgatory because there it is punished totally, but mortal sin cannot be said to be remitted after this life, because it is never punished there totally, unless in this world the guilt of eternal punishment were changed into the guilt of temporal punishment, and so here the remission would begin, he will not be able to be purged there. This opinion is false, both because without any doubt sin remains in man apart from the guilt of punishment, even a stain, or something similar, through which a man is formally called a sinner and worthy of punishment, and also because in this mode venial sins really cannot be said to be remitted in Purgatory, for that which is totally punished is not remitted, for remission denotes the gift.

There is another opinion of the same Scotus (*ibid.*), that venial sins are remitted in the first instant of the separation of the soul from the body, but remitted by preceding merits. For he says that every good work which pleases God more than venial sins displease him, thereupon remit venial sins; moreover, while a man lives, not all venial sins are remitted by good works of this sort, because the very pleasure taken in sin is an impediment which, once it has been lifted (which happens in the first instant after death), then sin is remitted. I don't like this because it is not probable that every good work remits venial sin, unless there were at least a virtual displeasure for those sins. Then, because it would follow that after this life sin is never remitted except one sin, namely the one whose act is continued even to death, that which Scotus himself admits, but it is against the Scripture and the Fathers, as is clear from the aforesaid. Thirdly, it would not be necessary to pray for the dead so that they would be absolved of venial sins, as the Church prays and from the prayers of the Church wherein we ask that what was contracted by human frailty be forgiven. (Dionysius, *Eccles. Hierarch.*, last chapter).

Therefore, the opinion of St. Thomas in 4, dist. 21, q. 1, art. 2 is true, that venial sins are forgiven in Purgatory by an act of love and patience; for that welcoming of punishment inflicted by God, since it proceeds from charity, can be called a certain virtual penance, and although it is not properly meritorious, because there is no increase of glory or grace, nevertheless, it does remit penance.

Ad Primum: I deny the major proposition universally, for it has place only in mortal sin;, what attains to venial sins, a soul can be freed from venial sins in Purgatory because it has appropriate means, *i.e.* an act of love contrary to sin, but it cannot fall into venial sin, because it lacks the *fomes peccati*, and besides, because it is confirmed in good.

Ad Secundum: I say after this life there is no penance for mortal sins, because the damned are fixed in evil, and Damascene holds this opinion, still in the souls of Purgatory there can rightly be displeasure at sin, and by that charity, and hence useful.

Ad Tertium: I say the souls of purgatory are not altogether on the road, and besides, they cannot merit an increase of grace; nevertheless, they are not altogether at the end, and therefore can do something which would pertain to the remission of venial sin.

I respond to the second part of the argument, the punishment depends upon the sin it happened in, not *in esse*, and therefore that phrase, "as the sin decreases so the punishment", if something were understood in which a sin is lesser in that it generates a lesser punishment, is true, otherwise it is false, for punishment is also due on account of a past fault.

CHAPTER XV
The Confession of Purgatory Pertains to the Catholic Faith

NOW it remains that we bring to naught the opinion of Peter Martyr, who, in his commentary on chapter 3 of 1 Corinthians, contends that the existence of Purgatory cannot pertain to a dogma of faith in any way, which was the first opinion of Luther, or perhaps his first error. There are five reasons for this.

1) *The first* reason is because Scripture is silent on Purgatory in those passages where there was the best occasion for speaking about it. In Genesis 49 the funerals of Abraham, Isaac, Jacob, Sarah and Rachel are very carefully described, and still not even a word is said about Purgatory. Likewise, in Leviticus, many kinds of sacrifices are instituted for different things, and there nothing is instituted for the dead. Next, Paul, in 1 Thessalonians 4, when he expressly argues about the dead, says nothing about Purgatory, but only asserts that they are going to rise and concludes: "Console each other with these words."

2) *The second* reason is because the Greek Church, which is the other part of the Church, resisted this doctrine for a long time in the Council of Florence, therefore, if even to our times half the Church does not believe Purgatory, how is it an article of faith?

3) *The third* reason is, because Dionysius, in the last chapter of *Ecclesiast. hierarchiae*, proposes this question: Why do Bishops in the burial of the faithful, pray for the dead and yet do not call purgatory to mind, and he labors anxiously to solve the question. But if Purgatory were a

dogma of faith, he could have easily responded right away that he prays for the dead so they would be freed from Purgatory.

4) *The fourth* reason is that St. Augustine asserts with precise language, that he had only an uncertain rather than certain trust that Purgatory exists, in *Enchiridion*, cap. 69, where he says: "That such a thing as that happens after this life does not seem unbelievable. It is a matter that may be inquired into, and either ascertained or left hidden, whether some believers will pass through a sort of purgatorial fire, and in proportion as they have loved with more or less devotion transitory goods, be less or more quickly delivered from it." In his book on eight questions of Dulcitius, quaest. 1, he says: "Whether in this life only, men suffer such things, or whether some such judgments also follow after this life, the meaning that I have given of this sentence, as I suppose, does not abhor the truth."

He says the same thing in *de fide et operibus*, cap. 16. Then, in book 21 of *City of God*, c. 26, he says: "But if it be said that in the interval of time between the death of this body and that last day of judgment and retribution which shall follow the resurrection, the bodies of the dead shall be exposed to a fire of such a nature that it shall not affect those who have not in this life indulged in such pleasures and pursuits as shall be consumed like wood, hay, stubble, but shall affect those others who have carried with them structures of that kind; if it be said that such worldliness, being venial, shall be consumed in the fire of tribulation either here only, or here and hereafter both, or here that it may not be hereafter — this I do not contradict, because possibly it is true."

5) *The fifth* reason is because Scripture clearly disagrees with it, as John 5, Luke 13 and Apocalypse 14, as we advanced and refuted above.

These are the mainstay of it and they do not move us at all, so that we resolutely again assert that Purgatory is a dogma of faith, so much so that one who does not believe that Purgatory exists will never arrive there, rather he is going to be tortured in the fire of hell. Now it is customarily proven as a dogma of faith in four ways.

Firstly, from the express testimony of Scripture with a declaration of the Church, in the way we prove that Chris is ὁμούσιον with the Father from that of John 10: "The Father and I are one," with the addition of the Council of Nicaea; for otherwise the quarrel with the Arians could not have been ended, since that passage, and others which they usually advanced they would explain otherwise.

Secondly, by the evident deduction from those which are expressly held in Scripture; in the way we prove Christ has two wills, divine and human, because according to the Scriptures, he is God and man, with the addition of the decree of the Sixth Council.

Thirdly, from the word of God not written by the Apostles, but handed down, in the way we prove the Gospels and the Epistles of Paul are divine Scriptures.

Fourthly, by the evident deduction from the word of God handed down, how St. Augustine everywhere proves that it must be believed that infants have original sin, even if it is not contained in Scripture because it is evidently deduced from Apostolic Tradition on infant Baptism. From that it is clear the sufficiency of these four modes is clear, because that alone is of the faith which has been revealed by God mediately or immediately. Moreover, divine revelations are partly written, and partly unwritten. Consequently, the decrees of Councils, Popes and the consent of doctors and all others are reduced to these four, for only then do they make a matter *de fide*, when they explain the word of God or deduce something from it.

Indeed, Purgatory is proven from all of these modes. From the first mode it is clear from twenty passages of Scripture, which we have advanced, and some of which are explained by the whole Church to be on Purgatory, as is clear from the Councils and the Fathers whom we cited.

In regard to the second mode, it is clear from the first two reasons which we gave.

On the third mode it is evident from the fact that we do not find the beginning of this doctrine, but all the Greek and Latin Fathers from the time of the Apostles constantly taught that there is a Purgatory. For such things must be related to Apostolic tradition, as St. Augustine affirms (lib. 4 *de Baptismo contra Donatistas*, cap. 24).

On the fourth mode it is clear from Clement, Tertullian, Epiphanius, and Chrysostom cited above, because they assert that prayer for the dead is Apostolic tradition, and none of the Fathers ever said the contrary. From that, it is evidently gathered that there is a Purgatory. If tradition is Apostolic, that it is necessary to pray for the dead, who does not see that it follows thence that souls after this life need assistance and hence they will not suffer eternal, but only temporal punishments? Nor will it be difficult for us to answer the arguments of Peter Martyr.

1) Therefore, to the first I respond: *firstly* it is not necessary for Scripture to say all things everywhere.

I say *secondly*, to that of Genesis that it was not an occasion of placing the doctrine on Purgatory. Genesis is not a book of dogmas, but a certain history of the Patriarchs. Thus, doctrine in that time is not preserved in Scripture but in tradition. Otherwise, we will say that before the times of Abraham no one was ever justified because Scripture does not hand down how men were justified in the time of Adam, Enoch and Noah.

Lastly, I say that mention of Purgatory is at least implicitly made in Genesis, for when it is said in Genesis 23 "And Abraham rose from the office of the funeral," what prevents that word, office (*officium*) from being taken to mean not only tears, but also prayer and fasting? And why, I ask, when Jacob and Joseph were dying in Egypt, they desired their bones to be brought into the promised land, except because there alone they knew sacrifices were going to be offered for the dead?

To that of Leviticus, I deny that sacrifices were not instituted for the dead in Leviticus, seeing that those which were instituted for sins were understood for the sins of both the living and the dead, which is clear from 2 Maccabees 12.

To that of Paul I say, that in that passage Paul only means to say one should not immoderately weep for the dead in the way the pagans do. Given his scope, however, it would not be of no benefit to his purpose, but even harm it to make mention of purgatory. For, to say the souls of our neighbors are severely tortured in Purgatory is not to advance matter for consolation, but greater mourning; Paul, however, meant to console them, as is clear, and therefore he mentioned the resurrection and glory and concludes: "Therefore, console one another with these words." But in other places, as earlier in 1 Corinthians 3:15 as well as chapter 15, and Hebrews 10, Paul precisely places the fire of Purgatory and the laborious baptism received for the dead.

2) I say to the second that the Greek Church never doubted about Purgatory, as is clear from the Fathers we have cited, Dionysius the Areopagate, Origen, Athanasius, Basil, Gregory Nazianzen, Gregory of Nyssa, Ephraim, Chrysostom, Cyril, Epiphanius, Theodoret, Oecumenius, Theophylactus, Damascene, and the Council of Florence itself. For, what Peter Martyr says, that in that Council the Greek Fathers resisted for a long time, is a lie, accordingly in the first session, and again in the last, they affirmed that they always believed in Purgatory as well as prayers for the dead, but only called into question the nature of the punishment, whether it is fire or something else. So what he boasts about the Greeks is either absolutely false or must be understood to be about individuals.

3) I marvel at the third argument of Peter Martyr, for even if Dionysius does not say Purgatory by name, nevertheless he expressly says that prayer is made for the dead to free them from sins. "With prayers he directs, by divine goodness, that all sins which were committed from human frailty would be forgiven to a man once he leaves this life." Next, he asks why prayer is made for the dead, so that his sins would be remitted, since it was written that all are going to receive insofar as they acted in their body? He answers therefore, they are prayed for, because they are made worthy by the merits of this life for the prayers of the living to benefit them. Even if St. Dionysius opposed himself, he could not ignore Purgatory or deny it since he so clearly asserted prayer for the sins of the dead.

4) To the fourth, we oppose other citations of St. Augustine. In the same Enchiridion, c. 110, he asserts that prayers and sacrifices benefit souls and similarly in quaest. 2 *ad Dulcitium*, as well as *City of God* book 21, ch. 24, he says it is certain that souls are cleansed after this life, and in chapter 1 *de Cura pro mortuis*, he says: "There is no doubt that prayer benefitted the dead."

Peter Martyr responds that these passages ought to be explained by those in which he doubts. But how, I ask, will we explain "it is certain," and "there is no doubt," by "It is not unbelievable" and "Perhaps it is true"? It is necessary to say that Augustine held something about Purgatory with certain faith, and doubted on some matter. What exactly he doubted we will easily explain. But Peter Martyr will not so easily be able to explain what it is on which Augustine did not doubt, for nothing less can be granted than that he had not doubts about purgatory in general, *i.e.* that there is some purgatory after this life. With some certain faith, doubt could exist on the type of punishment which is inflicted, on the nature of the sin which is punished in the place, the time, etc. Yet, no certain faith in regard to purgatory can correspond with uncertainty about Purgatory in general; nevertheless, Augustine says he has certain faith in regard to it.

Therefore, I say that Augustine, in those four citations, only doubts on the type of sin which is punished, namely, whether it is like immoderate love toward temporal things in this life which is purged by God through various afflictions, such as the death of a wife and children, etc. So also it would be believable, after this life, for certain other relics of such actual affections which ought to be cleansed by tribulations and troubles to still remain in the disembodied spirit. Even if disembodied spirits do not seem to be able to be touched by corporal affections of this sort, nevertheless, when they are forms of bodies and were in the body for a long time as well as desire to be reunited with the body, it is not unbelievable that they still remember the desire which they experienced through corporeal instruments and thereby hold onto some desire. But because the matter is so difficult, Augustine rightly said it could be inquired after and perhaps the answer would never found.

5) The fifth has already been answered above.

END BOOK I

BOOK II
ON THE CIRCUMSTANCES OF PURGATORY

CHAPTER I
On the Persons for whom Purgatory is Suited

ITHERTO, it has been shown that Purgatory exists. Now we must treat the genus on the circumstances of Purgatory, *i.e.* on the persons, the place, time, punishments, prayers and other matters.

The first question that arises is: "For which persons is purgation after this life suited?" There are many errors extant on the persons of this kind.

1) *The first* was that both the good and the bad need to be purged after this life, with the exception of Christ. This opinion is usually attributed to Alcuin, but it seems to be not only his, but of several Fathers. Origen (*hom. 14 in Lucam*) says: "I think that after the resurrection from the dead we will need the sacrament to wash and also cleanse us, for no man could rise again without spot, nor could any soul be found that would not have any vices." And on Psalm 36 (37) he says: "It is necessary for all of us to come to that fire, even if someone were Paul or Peter."

St. Ambrose, on Psalm 36 (37) says: "The sons of Levi will be cleansed in fire, Ezechiel and Daniel by fire." And in Psalm 118 (119), serm. 20, adducing that of Genes. 4 "He placed before paradise a fiery sword," says that the fiery sword is the purgatorial fire, through which whoever would pass into paradise necessarily must pass through the fire. "It is necessary for all to make passage through the flames, whether he was John or Peter, etc." And further, "The one Christ of God, who is justice, could not feel that fire."

Hilary seems to have supposed the same thing from the words of Psalm 118 (119) "My soul eagerly longs for the judgments of your justice." There he even insinuates that the Blessed Virgin ought to pass through the fire. Lactantius held the same thing (lib. 7 cap. 21 *divin. Instit.*) and Jerome, in ch. 7 of Amos, from those words: "Behold he will call the fire to judgment." Next, Rupert (lib. 3 *in Genes.* c. 32) explaining the fire sword.

This opinion, taken as it sounds, contains a manifest error. For in the last session of the Council of Florence, it was defined that some souls are received in hell, some in purgatory, some in heaven. Next, the Church believes those who die right after Baptism can never suffer the punishment of Purgatory, as Augustine firmly teaches (*de Civitate Dei*, lib. 21, cap. 16) and likewise those who are Baptized in blood, as Cyprian says (lib. 4, epist. 2), for he affirms all sins are cleansed in martyrdom, therefore, martyrs immediately obtain their reward.

Additionally, what the Fathers adduced (with the exception of Origen, whose words in *hom. 14 in Lucam* do not suffer a suitable exposition) seem to be able to be understood in a sound mode: for some of them do not understand the fire to be a purgatorial fire, but the fire of divine judgment, in the way Paul speaks in 1 Corinthians 3, when he says: "Fire will prove the value of the work of each and every man." And in this mode it must be affirmed that all the Saints, with the exception of Christ, made passage through the fire. It seems in this way that Hilary and Jerome spoke about the fire, and in the later passage Ambrose.

But some seem to understand the fire to be the true flame of Purgatory, through which they say the Saints pass

Ch. I: Those for whom Purgatory is fitting

through without any harm, so that they would pass through Purgatory materially, but not formally. This is the way it seems Lactantius, Ambrose and Rupert speak. Lactantius so says: "But also, when God judges the just and will have already examined them with fire, then for those whose sins prevail either by weight or number, they will be bound to the fire and burned; but those who are full of justice and whom the ripeness of virtue has smelted, they will not perceive the fire, for they have something in them of God which repels the force of the flame." So also Ambrose speaks in Psalm 36 (27), where he had said all are going to pass through the fire, he added that certain men are going to remain in the fire perpetually, certain men must be burned, but still it is not going to burn certain me, *i.e.* the saints, after the fashion of dew, just as it was for the three children in the furnace at Babylon.

The vision of St. Fursaeus conforms to this opinion, which St. Bede describes (lib. 3 *historiae*, cap. 19). He saw on the road to heaven great fires, through which one had to pass, but at the same time saw those who had nothing burnable, *i.e.* no sin or punishment to suffer and they passed unharmed, but others were more or less burned precisely as they carried burnable matter. Taken in this way, I do not dare to assert that the opinion teaching all are going to pass through the fire, although not all are harmed by it should be held as true, nor condemn it as an error.

2) *The second* error, is that all the wicked, and the demons, will at length escape hell and be altogether saved, and hence all punishments after this life are purgatorial. This error was of Origen, as Epiphanius relates and refutes in his epistle to John of Jerusalem, Augustine (*de Civitate*

Dei, lib. 21, cap. 17 & 23), Jerome (c. 3 *Jonae*), and Gregory (*moral.* lib. 9, cap. 45 & 45, and book 34, cap. 12 & 13). For in Matthew 25 it is said: "Go, ye accursed, into the eternal fire which has been prepared for the devil and his angels." And lest someone would answer that the fire is eternal, but a dwelling does not remain in the fire, the Lord concludes: "These will go into eternal punishment, but the just into eternal life." And in Apocalypse 20, "The devil, who seduced them, was sent into the lake of fire and sulfur, where the beast and the false-prophets will be tortured day and night in ages of ages."

Ruffinus attributed the same error to St. Jerome (lib. 1 *invectio in Hieronymum*), but this was an injury, for St. Jerome was very bitterly opposed to this error, which is clear from the place we recently cited, and from *Apolog.* 2 *contra Ruffinum*, from book 1 *contra Pelagionos*, from the epistle to Pammachius, on the errors of John of Jerusalem, and from the commentary on the last words of Isaiah. The things that Ruffinus cites as an error from Jerome's commentary on Ephesians were said in the person of Origen, as Jerome teaches on similar errors in *Apologia* 1 *contra Ruffinum*. It is related that a book of a certain Anabaptist named Stanislaus favors this error of Origen, which is titled *De Divina Philanthropia*; but I have not yet been able to see the book.

3) *The third* error is of those who hold that the punishments of all sinful men, though not the devil, will be purgatorial after this life, as Augustine relates and refutes in *de Civitate Dei*, lib. 21, c. 18 and 24.

4) *The fourth* error is of those who thought the number of those in Purgatory will be made up only of Christians,

Ch. I: Those for whom Purgatory is fitting   143

whether heretics or Catholics; Augustine relates this also (*Ibid.*, cap. 19 and 25).

5) *The fifth* error is of those who thought it was on only those and all those who at one time were Catholic. (Augustine, *ibid.* c. 20 and 25). This error is refuted not only from Matthew 25: "Go into the eternal fire," and Apocalypse 20, "They will be tortured for ages of ages," but even from the last of Isaiah: "Their fire will not be extinguished," and Galatians 5: "Those who do such things will never possess the kingdom of God." For in these passages it is said that not only will demons or pagans, or heretics be punished without end, but even dissolute Catholics.

There were four foundations for this error. The *first*, because Psalm 76 (77) says: "God will never forget to be merciful, nor will he hold back mercy in his wrath?" *Second*, because in Romans 11 it says: "God concealed all in infidelity so that he might have mercy on all."

Third, because if the Saints prayed for their enemies, and were heard in this life, they will pray much more and be heard on the day of judgment. *Fourth*, because we see in the Scripture that God absolutely threatens punishments and still, later they are not imposed, as is clear from Jonah 3: "After forty days, and Niniveh will be destroyed." For this reason, we understand, they say, when God threatens punishments, it does not mean they really are imposed, but only from those whom are threatened, those worthy are punished in this way.

St. Augustine responds to the *first* in *de Civitate Dei*, lib. 21, cap. 25, that these words are understood in respect to the good, or if they were extended to the damned, the sense is: the damned are indeed going to be punished forever, but not as much as they deserve. It could also be said that those words are understood in this life, on which it is said: "Behold, now is the acceptable time," for on the coming judgment James speaks: "Judgment without mercy for the man that does not show mercy."

Augustine responds to the second (*ibid.*), that the verse: "So that he would have mercy on all," does not mean all men, but every nation, that is both of the Gentiles and of the Jews, so that some from the Gentiles and some from the Jews will be saved, while the verse, "He concealed all in infidelity," means both the Gentiles and the Jews, that is, some from the Gentiles and some from the Jews, for before the arrival of Christ God permitted the Gentiles to go out on their path in infidelity and idolatry, so that later the confused would require a doctor, and would find him, just as it came to pass. Then after the Gentiles converted, he permitted infidelity to ruin the Jews, so that they will be confused and humbled until the end of the world, when they will be converted.

He responds to the *third*, that the saints in this world prayed because they knew in this life the time for fruitful penance is short, but in judgment they are not going to pray for the damned, just as now we do not pray for the devil and the other damned.

Augustine responds to the *fourth*, Nineveh was truly overturned as it has been predicted, for all the men changed from wicked to good, which is the best overturning, because it was understood conditionally, unless someone would doe penance, but after this life it is not penance, at least fruitful penance, but after this life there is no fruitful penance, for John 9 says: "Work while it is day; night is coming, in which no man can work." And in Ecclesiastes 9: "In hell there is no work, or reason, etc."

6) *The sixth* error is of others who would have it that all and only Catholics persevering in faith descend to Purgatory, even if otherwise they lived the worst possible life. Augustine relates and refutes this error (*de Civitate Dei*, lib. 21, c. 25 and 26; *Enchirid.* c. 68; *de fide et operibus*, c. 15-16; Quaest. 1 *ad Dulcitium*). For in Matthew 3 it is said about the wicked faithful: "But he will burn the chaff with an inextinguishable fire." And in Matthew 25 it will be said to the pitiless: "Go into the eternal fire." And in 1 Corinthians 6, Paul writes, "Neither drunkards nor the greedy, nor adulterers, nor the effeminate, nor those cursing will possess the kingdom of God." And we find similar things in Galatians 5 and Ephesians 5.

The foundation of this error was that passage of 1 Cor. 3:15, "But he will be saved, as if by fire," for they thought by foundation the Catholic faith was meant, by silver and gold all good works, by wood, grass and hay all sins, but this was sufficiently refuted in chapter 5 of the last book.

Moreover, we must observe that there are some who thought St. Jerome labored in this error, because in the last words of Isaiah he says: "Just as we believe the devil and all apostates and the impious who said in their heart, 'There is no God,' will go to eternal torments, so also we think the sentence of the merciful judge mixed and moderate that the works of sinners and also the pious, and still of Christians, must be proven and purged in the fire." Likewise in book 1 *contra Pelagianos*: "If Origen says all rational creatures do not perish what is there for us? Don't we say the devil and his angels and all the impious perish perpetually? But Christians, if they were first in sin, can be saved after punishment."

Nevertheless, it seems to some that Jerome held to this error, seeing that in chapter 25 of Matthew where it is manifestly a question of the eternal damnation of the faithful who are sinners, he so writes: "O prudent reader, attend, that the punishments are also eternal, and thus, eternal life does not have the fear of ruin." And in c. 4 to the Galatians, he remarks: "Do we think we obtain the kingdom of God if we are free from fornication, idolatry and sorcery? Look to enmity, contention, wrath, quarrelling, dissension, also drunkenness and the rest which we account as nothing, exclude us from the kingdom of God."

In the cited passages to the contrary, St. Jerome does not mean to say that all Christians are saved after penalties, but that none but Christians are saved after penalties. Wherefore, in the earlier passage he did say that impious Christians are saved, but he added a restrictive condition, when he says: "Whose works are going to be purged in fire, and have been purged," *i.e.* only those impious Christians will be saved whose wicked works have already been purged, in regard to sin, will be cleansed insofar as they suffer punishments. In the later citation, he opposes Christians to the impious, who are found in deadly sin, since he indicates that he is only speaking about pious Christians.

7) *The seventh* error is of those who think everyone who gives alms will be saved by the fire of Purgatory, even if they otherwise persevered in sin even to death.

St. Augustine refutes this error (*Enchirid.* c. 75 and 76; *de Civitate Dei*, lib. 21, c. 22 and 27). He says that Scripture requires many things with the clearest words for the justification of the impious apart from almsgiving. In Luke 13:5, it says "If you will not have done penance, you will all perish likewise," and 1 Corinthians 13:3, "If I will spend all my powers in giving food to the poor, but would not have charity, it is of no benefit to me." Who, I ask, has the sort of charity that would not fear to offend God, or after offending him, would not seek reconciliation? But, they say, after examination is made on the day of judgment, we see only about almsgiving (Matthew 25), those who gave alms are sent into the kingdom, but those who did not are sent to hell. *I respond:* The Lord posited lesser things so that we would gather greater things from it. He threatens hell to those who did not give their own things, to punish them more than those who took the goods of others; and he promised the kingdom to those who gave alms from their own money, to crown much more those who lay down their life for the sake of faith. See, if you would, the many things in our disputation *On Almsgiving*.[9]

So, with these errors confuted, the last true and Catholic opinion remains: Purgatory is only for those who die with venial sins, which is the matter at hand in 1 Corinthians 3:12 *et seqq.* For they are those who build upon a foundation with wood and straw, and will be saved as if by fire. And again for those who fall deserving punishment, whose sins have already been forgiven, which is the subject of Luke 12:59: "You will not go out from there until you have paid the last penny," and in the other passages cited in the previous book.

---

[9] Tomus III, *de Gratia, libero arbitrio et justificatione*, on good works in particular, book 3. This will be forthcoming from Mediatrix Press.

CHAPTER II
In Purgatory, Souls can Neither Gain Merit nor Sin

NOTHER question follows. Is there a place for merit and sin in Purgatory? Luther, when he confessed Purgatory, did so in this way: it is mixed partly with the state of this life and partly with hell. He said that the souls of Purgatory can merit, which is of this life, and again, that they can both sin on the spot and despair of salvation, which are proper to the damned. The root of these was that he thought the souls are sent to purgatory that were not perfected in charity; those having no charity are sent into hell, those with perfect charity, ascend into heaven. On the other hand, imperfect charity ought to be increased, and it cannot be increased without new merits, therefore, he placed a state of merit in Purgatory; again, because perfect charity sends fear out of doors, and hence imperfect charity is mixed with fear, and is clearly servile, and from here Luther thought fear is a sin; thence he deduces that souls sin because they fear, shudder and flee punishment, they seek what is their own, etc. See the book of Luther on Purgatory, which John Eck refuted.[10]

That this opinion of Luther is also manifestly heretical is proven by the testimonies of the Scriptures and of the Fathers. 1) From Sirach 9:5: "The dead knew nothing more,

---

[10] Translator's note: It is not certain here which book "on Purgatory" that Bellarmine is referring to that was refuted by Eck. Luther's early writings do profess belief in Purgatory as Bellarmine lays it out here, but in 1530 Luther clearly rejected it altogether in his tract *Revocation of Purgatory*.

nor have any further reward." Jerome says on this passage: "So long as they live, men can become just, but after death they no longer have an occasion for good works... Living with the fear of death they can carry out good works, but the dead do not have the power to add to that which they once had when they have died... Nor can they act justly, or sin, or add virtues and vices."

2) In the same place, verse 10, Scripture says: "Whatever your hand can do, act urgently because neither work nor reason nor wisdom is in hell, where you hasten." We cannot say in another life nothing is done or known, since in Luke 16:23 we read about the rich man, that he also saw Lazarus in the bosom of Abraham and implored the assistance of Abraham first for himself, then for his brethren; this is why he speaks about meritorious work, as St. Jerome explains, and he is not speaking about the lower hell, but on hell *in genere*, as it embraces all places to which all men descended before the resurrection of Christ.

3) *The third* passage is Sirach 11:3, "If a tree will fall either to the north or to the south, wherever it will have fallen, there it shall lie." Jerome as well as St. Bernard, commenting on this passage (*sermon.* 49), explain that this is said in regard to the immutability of the soul after this life, which cannot go from wicked to good or good to wicked.

4) The *fourth* passage is Sirach 14:17, "Before your death do justice, because in hell there is no food to find."

5) *The fifth* passage is Sirach 18:22, "Do not fear to be justified even to death." Why even to death? Except because after death there will be no more time.

6) *The sixth* passage is John 9:4, "Night comes, during which no man works." Origen (Psalm 36), Chrysostom,

Augustine, Euthymius, and Theophylactus (on this passage), as well as Jerome and Gregory (*Dialog*. lib. 4 c. 39), unanimously explain that "night" means the time of the next life; for "to work", is meant to do meritorious works.

7) *The seventh* is 2 Corinthians 5:10, "We must all be made manifest before the tribunal of Christ so that each man might receive what is proper of the body, as he did, whether good or evil." Augustine, explaining this place (*de praedest. Sanctorum*, c. 12) adverts that what is proper of the body is not called corporal works, as if spiritual things were not going to be judged, but rather means all works which are done while we are in the body, because after this life no time remains to work, rather, to receive reward or punishment.

8) *The eighth* passage is Galatians 6:8-10, "As a man will have sown, he will also reap... But let us not fail doing good, for unfailing we will reap in season, therefore, while we have time, let us do good." Jerome teaches on this passage that the time to sow is not extended beyond this life, rather, to sow is to work well.

9) *The ninth* passage is Luke 16:2, "Give an account of your stewardship, for you cannot be a steward any longer." St. Ambrose, Theophylactus, Jerome (q. 6 *ad Algasiam*), Augustine (*de Civitate Dei*, lib. 21, c. 7) and all others understand death by the deposing from stewardship, and by the fact he can no longer be steward, that one can no longer merit and profit.

10) *the tenth* is Apocalypse 10:6. The Angel having one foot over the sea and the other over the land, swears by the living in ages of ages that there will be no more time, namely *to do good.* Then, Scripture everywhere witnesses

Ch. II: The souls in Purgatory cannot merit

this, and a syllable will never be found favoring the error of Luther.

Secondly, it is proven from the Fathers. Cyprian (*Sermon 4*, which is on mortality) says death is a great benefit for this purpose, that we might be delivered from the danger of sin. For, while we are in this life, we fight in the arena, death brings the end of the battle. Augustine, when adding that passage of Cyprian, adds: "By these and such like sentiments, that teacher sufficiently and plainly witnesses in the clearest light of the Catholic faith, that perils of sin as well as trials are to be feared even until this body has been laid aside, but that afterwards no one shall suffer any such things. And even if he did not testify thus, when could any manner of Christian be in doubt on this matter?" (*de praedest. Sanctorum*, c. 14).

Note that Luther cannot be called a Christian in any way based on Augustine's opinion, rather, clearly a heathen, since he is uncertain on the matter which Augustine says no Christian can be uncertain of. Augustine says the same thing in the Enchiridion (cap. 110), "Therefore, here all merit is earned, which can relieve or aggravate... but no man then, may hope for himself when he has died that he shall obtain merit with God which he has neglected here."

Chrysostom (hom. 2 *de Lazaro*) says many things on this opinion, and in hom. 37 in Matthew, he says: "This present life granted the power to you to live rightly and vice versa; but after your day you will die, and consequently undergo judgment and penalty." Jerome (*In Eccles.* 9) says: "The dead cannot act justly or sin." Damascene (*de fide Orthodoxa*, lib. 2 cap. 4) says: "What the fall was to the Angels, death is the same to men."

Thirdly, it is proved from reason: Luther's opinion opposes itself. For Luther says these souls may and must merit because they are imperfect in charity, namely that perfect charity is increased by new merits. He says the same thing, that those souls, because they are imperfect, fear punishment and sin in that fear, and because they are always afraid while they are imperfect, hence they also always sin while they are imperfect.

But these are interiorly opposed. For a man that sins, particularly a mortal sin, cannot merit while he sins. Yet, if these souls always sin while they are in Purgatory, because they are imperfect, consequently, they can never merit while they are in Purgatory. Besides, in the second place, because it follows it is impossible to free souls from Purgatory, for they will always sin while they are afraid; they will always be imperfect until a new charity will be added to them; a new charity cannot be added to them except by merits; they cannot merit while they sin, therefore they will never be freed.

CHAPTER III
Objections are Answered

It remains now to answer arguments.

1) The *first argument*: The souls which abide in Purgatory are imperfect in charity, therefore they ought to effect and merit that they would be made perfect. *Firstly*, if these souls were perfect, certainly they would not be punished since, to what end would perfect spirits be punished? If one were to say to make satisfaction to God, it could be answered that they especially make satisfaction to God by charity, as "Charity covers a multitude of sins," as St. Peter teaches (1 Peter 4:8).

Secondly, because if someone dies, if he still were to have a debt for ten days of fasting, and still supremely loved God, it is incredible that God would not forgive him those ten days since God customarily freely receives the will where he does not find the means; therefore, if his debt is not forgiven, it is a sign that he was not perfect in charity.

Thirdly, because if they were perfect, they would not fear punishments; for perfect charity sends fear out of doors. If they would not fear punishments, they will not be punished because a penalty is not that which is loved, and freely received; therefore they would not be in Purgatory unless they were imperfect.

Fourthly, because nothing can be perfect outside of God, according to that of 1 Corinthians 13:10, "When that which is perfect will have come, that which is but a part will be purged." Therefore, the souls of Purgatory which are not blessed, are necessarily imperfect. Then, the consequents of the first argument are proven.

a) It is impossible to stand in the road, it is always necessary to go forward or back, as Bernard says, but the souls of Purgatory are on the road and have not yet arrived; *b)* "Virtue is perfected in infirmity," (2 Corinthians 12:9), and gold is brightened in the furnace; *c)* it is impossible for some creature to be preserved except that he would always receive more and more until it would be absorbed in its source, just as happens in rivers which always receive new water until they enter the sea; for this reason, life is usually described as a type of continuous creation; *d)* charity after this life will be greater, therefore it will be increased, therefore that happens by merits.

I respond to the preceding: The souls of Purgatory can be called imperfect in respect to those which are in glory, and even a soul in Purgatory can be called imperfect in respect to another, whether in Purgatory or existing in this world. Nevertheless, every soul existing absolutely in Purgatory is perfected in charity. For there is no charity that is simply imperfect: "He who keeps his word, truly in him the charity of God has been perfected" (1 John 2:5). Moreover, each degree of charity suffices that someone would keep the word, that is, the precepts of the Lord.

To the consequent I say that the souls of Purgatory, insofar as they are imperfect in respect to souls in heaven, ought to be perfected in charity; but that increase does not require new merits, for it will be the reward of all past merits. Charity is increased in two ways: in one mode, in a kind of grace, that a man would become more suitable to merit more, and this increase is not granted after this life; in the other mode, in a kind of glory, so that a reward is given for all past merits, and this will take place in beatitude itself. For a part of the reward will be such copious charity that a man could never be deprived of beatitude and justice, who will have been provided with this copious charity, as Augustine says (*de correptione et gratia*, lib. 2 cap. 10).

Now, let us respond to the objections in order. I say to the *first* that by charity satisfaction is not properly made, rather by the sorrow commanded by charity, and whatever can be done so that the sorrow intended were of such a kind, and proceeding from such a charity that it would fully make satisfaction for every crime. Nevertheless, it can also happen that the sorrow were not such and on that account something would remain to be cleansed in Purgatory; for, punishment that must be undergone to make satisfaction which takes place outside of the kingdom of heaven is not opposed to the perfection of charity. To the words of St. Peter, I say that charity covers a multitude of sins, but not in the same mode in regard to sin and punishment; for it blots out the whole sin by its act, but it does not always abolish the punishment by its whole act, rather by satisfactory works which charity itself demands.

To the second, I say likewise: if someone dies and he suffers for his sins with supreme love, he can in that mode make satisfaction for every sin; but if his sorrow is not very great, he ought to make satisfaction later in Purgatory. Nor is it opposed that he might desire to fast, if he would remain alive. God does receive the will where he does not find the means, for in that the means of making satisfaction is found, if not in fasting, certainly by suffering in Purgatory.

To the third, I say that the soul in Purgatory does not fear, rather really suffers punishments. Fear is of future things, not the present. Besides, I say that fear of punishment is not opposed to perfect charity, otherwise Christ, who feared punishments, and from that fear sweated blood (Luke 22:44), was not perfected in charity. But what John says: "Perfect charity sends fear out of doors," is not understood in regard to fear of punishment, but the fear of sin, especially on account of punishment, for one that perfectly loves, fears to offend God, especially on account of God himself, not on account of the punishment which follows those offending God; likewise, perfect charity is free from that servile fear with which someone would not dare sin lest he be damned, so that he will sin if he does not fear damnation.

To the fourth, I say that outside of God nothing so perfect that would not be said to be imperfect in respect to *the perfection of glory* could be found; nevertheless, the thing itself will be perfect simply. This is why Paul says in Philippians 3:12, "I am not yet perfected, but I follow, if I may by any means apprehend." And further (verse 15): "Therefore, let us, as many have been made perfect." There, he says he is perfected absolutely, and still is imperfect in comparison to the blessed.

Now, to the first confirmation of the consequent, I say the souls of Purgatory are not on the road, but at the end, inasmuch as we consider an increase of grace. For a man that aims for some city, and arrives at its gates in the middle of the night is said to have arrived and completed the whole way, although he finds the gates closed and cannot enter until the sun rises. Besides, what Bernard says: "To not move forward on the way of God is to go back," ought not be received mathematically, but morally, for he does not mean to say in any work we merit an increase of grace or lose some grace, but they who do not pay attention to accomplish their purpose, can easily be impelled by the devil, and the world to fall., etc.

To the second confirmation, I say that in the first place Paul speaks about the virtue of God literally, which is said to be perfected in infirmity, because then the power of God appears the more that they resist it; for in Greek it is δύναμις μου, that is "my virtue." I say besides, our virtue is also perfected in tribulations, but only in this life, in regard to the true increase of virtue, because only in this life do we have the occasion to merit; but in the next it can be said to be perfected in Purgatory, not because something is added to him, but because the blight of sin is taken away; in the way that gold is made brighter in the furnace, not because something is added to it, but because it is separated from earth, lead and similar things.

I say to the third confirmation, that the principle of Luther in permanent matters is very false, and only has place *in successive* matter; otherwise permanent matters would never be the same and thus God would not now punish Judas in hell but one that sinned who was created after him. Nor would he have rewarded Peter who merited, but another man created later. But it is said that life is continual creation, which is true but what is understood to be created is that same thing, it does not increase or become something new.

The fourth has already been answered.

The *second argument* of Luther: Souls in Purgatory sin right away, therefore they are in a state of merit and demerit. He proves the antecedent: those souls abhor punishments, and they take refuge and seek rest; therefore, they sin. He proves the antecedent not only because otherwise they would not be punished (for a punishment ought to be involuntary and bitter), but also because we ought not to pray for their rest and liberation from Purgatory if they themselves love these punishments.

Thereupon he proves the consequent. 1) *Firstly*, all punishments become sweet to a man that loves them, therefore, those souls, while they flee punishments, do not perfectly love, hence they sin. 2) *Secondly*, because while they flee punishments, they seek their own honor, not God's. 3) *Thirdly*, because they love God with a love of concupiscence while they desire to be free from it. 4) *Fourthly*, because Christ says: "He that does not take up his cross is not worthy of me," *i.e.* a man that does not receive it freely and of his own will. But Purgatory is the cross of souls, so they sin while they flee that cross.

I respond: the souls in Purgatory abhor and flee punishments, and seek rest insofar as they consider these as evils and contrary to nature, and still at the same time they freely admit and tolerate them insofar as they consider them as instruments through which they are purged. In the same way, a sick man abhors bitter medicine, and still freely takes it because by it he hopes to be cured, nor can there ever be a sin in this. For the Lord, who could not sin, abhorred certain punishments, and said, "Father, take this chalice from me." (Matthew 26:39), and David declared: "Because I suffered tribulation, hear me speedily." (Psalm 68/69:18). And on Peter, Christ said: "When you grow old another will bind you, and lead you, whither you do not wish to go." (John 21:18).

Ch. III: Objections are answered

Next, St. Cyprian says in his work on mortality: "Who doesn't wish to be without sadness? Who does not hasten to embrace joy?" And St. Augustine, in book 10, chapter 28 of *Confessions*, says about punishments: "You ask us to endure them, not to love them, for no man loves that which he endures, although he loves to endure."

So, *to the first*, in which the consequence is proven, I say that punishments are not made so sweet to a lover that he does not perceive them, but so that although they are bitter, he nevertheless endures them eagerly on account of what is loved, which is clear both from the aforesaid, and from the words of St. Eleazar: "O Lord, who hast the holy knowledge, you clearly know that, whereas I might be delivered from death, I suffer grievous pains in body. Yet in soul, I am well content to suffer these things because I fear you." (2 Maccabees 6:30). And this was the common feeling of the martyrs who truly felt the most bitter sufferings and still gladly offered themselves, although God granted a privilege to certain men to remove the pain or some sense of it by abundance of consolation, as Ruffinus writes about St. Theodore (*histor.* lib. 10 cap. 36).

To the second, I say they do not seek what is their own, but the honor of God. For they desire to be liberated sooner so that they could praise God more and better.

To the third I say, they love God with the love of friendship because they refer their good to God.

To the fourth I say, they take up their cross because they freely suffer and do not desire to be freed except according to the will of God and by the means which God established. And certainly, if the things that Luther says were true, *i.e.* those souls seek that which are their own and that they love God with a love of concupiscence, they would neither take up their cross nor have even imperfect charity, rather they would have none and they should not be in Purgatory, but in hell.

Now, the *third* argument is of certain Catholics. The souls of Purgatory have everything necessary for merit, for they have grace, faith, hope, charity and free will, at least in regard to its exercise; so why don't they merit? *Then*, the blessed can merit, as is clear from Christ who was always blessed and still merited, consequently, how much more can the souls of Purgatory merit? *Likewise*, the rich man in hell prayed for himself and his own (Luke 16:24), therefore, even the souls of Purgatory could pray; but their prayer proceeds, without a doubt, from charity, so they merit to be heard. *Lastly*, they confirm the same with the authority of St. Thomas, who in 4, dist. 21, q. 1, a. 3 ad 4, says that after this life merit cannot be found in respect to essential reward, but only in respect to the accidental.

I respond to the argument: the *state of life* is lacking to the souls in purgatory in regard to merit; for God, as is clearly proven from the Scriptures, only constituted the period of this life to take up good works for merit or demerit. After this life good works will be the effect of glory and evil the effect of damnation.

To the first confirmation, I say that Christ was at the same time in possession of beatitude and a wayfarer, so on the side of a wayfarer he was able to merit, but after his death, since this state was lacking to him, he could merit no more.

To the second I say: If the souls of Purgatory would pray for themselves or us, (on which we will treat later in a question on suffrage), they do not merit, rather they only ask from past merits, in the way that now the Saints procure for us in prayer although they do not merit.

To the third confirmation, I say: St. Thomas changed his opinion; for in q. 7 of *de Malo*, article 11, he clearly teaches that in Purgatory there can be no merit, whether of essential or accidental reward. St. Bonaventure teaches the same thing, as do Scotus, Durandus and others. Perhaps even St. Thomas in the citation from the Sentences, meant to use the term "merit" not properly but *improperly*, for he called the act of delight in Purgatory meritorious for the remission of venial sin, because it is a remission, although not in the mode of merit properly so called, but by the mode of one thing abolishing its contrary.

CHAPTER IV
The souls in Purgatory are Certain about their Eternal Salvation

NOW, we must treat on the third question, whether souls in Purgatory are certain or not about their salvation?

Luther, in art. 38, teaches that they are not certain. Some Catholics teach the same thing, who think that there are different punishments in Purgatory, and one is the greatest of all, uncertainty of salvation, whereby they say certain souls are only punished, so although they really are certain of their salvation, sill they do not know this. So it seems Dennis the Carthusian thought, on account of certain visions which he relates in his book on the four last things, art. 47. Bajus teaches the same thing (*de merit. operum*, lib. 2 c. 8), where, wishing to prove that venial sin by its nature merits eternal death, adduces into argument that otherwise it would follow the souls in Purgatory are certain about their salvation, which seemed to be absurd to him.

Next, it seems the same thing is deduced from the teaching of Gerson (*lectione 1 de vita spirituali*) and John Fisher (*contra art. 32 Lutheri*), both of whom admit there is no such a thing as venial sin except by the mercy of God and hence it can be justly punished forever if God wills. So, it follows that souls having venial sins cannot know for certain whether they will be punished forever, although Fisher, in art. 38 of Luther, contends that the souls of

Ch. V: The souls in Purgatory are certain of salvation

Purgatory are certain about there salvation; but I do not see how that is consistent with his first opinion.

But the common teaching of theologians is that all souls which are in Purgatory have certitude about their salvation. Moreover, that it would be understood to what extent they have certitude, we must know that there are three degrees of certitude.

1) *The first* is that which excludes every hope and all fear, and such is of the blessed for whom beatitude is not some future thing, but the present life.

2) *The second* is that which excludes all fear, but not all hope, and such is in Purgatory; for beatitude is the future life for them, not the present, and therefore it does not remove the expectation; and again it is arduous because they attain it by punishments, and so their waiting can be called hope. Nevertheless, it is not contingent, but necessary, because they cannot lose anything more, and therefore it removes all fear.

3) *The third* is that which excludes neither hope nor fear and can be called a conjectural degree of certitude, and such is our lot. Beatitude is for us a future good and not a present; arduous and not easy, contingent and not necessary or impossible, and so we most properly hope and fear, as we are still in battle in the contest, in agony.

Now we shall show the matter to be so. If the souls [of Purgatory] do not have certitude of their salvation, necessarily it would happen on account of one of four reasons: either they could still merit and lose merit; they were not yet judged; they are ignorant of the sentence of the judge, even though it has been imposed; on account of the magnitude of their suffering they are so absorbed that their judgment is obscured to the extent that they cannot think of or see this certitude. But none of these have place. Not the first, as is clear; not the second, because although the universal judgment has not been made, still apart from it there is the particular judgment, in which souls are immediately judged from death, as the Theologians teach in 4 dist. 47, as well as St. Thomas in III pars, q. 59 art. 5.

They usually add for this purpose that the particular judgment is proven from two passages. One is that of John 5:22, "The father gave every judgment to the Son," for when he says "every judgment' it seems to mean many judgments; clearly one is particular and the other universal. The other is from Hebrews 9:27, "It has been established for men to die once, and after this, judgment." But those passages do not conclude the matter; both can be understood about universal judgment, for that "*omne*" of John 5 does not necessarily refer to two judgments, particular and general; but to judge different men and different works. The sense of the other passage from Hebrews 9:27 is: When all men are dead, then there will be judgment, as Oecumenius explains.

Nevertheless, the particular judgment is efficaciously proven from those words of Sirach 11:28, "It is easy to give back to each one in the presence of God on the day of death, according to his ways." Likewise, in verse 29: "At the end of man his works are laid bare."

Besides, the same is evidently gathered from another truth: It is *de fide* that soon after death the impious descend to eternal punishments, as is clear from Luke 16:22 about the rich man, and the just to eternal life; as is clear from Luke 23:43 about the thief, "Today you will be with me in paradise." But it is not in any way credible that God

Ch. V: The souls in Purgatory are certain of salvation 165

would distribute punishments and rewards before the judgment has been made.

Next, the Fathers teach the same thing. St. Cyprian, in his sermon on mortality, says: "We must rejoice and embrace the reward of time, since while we firmly display our faith, and while enduring the labor continue to Christ through the narrow road of Christ, we take the reward of life and faith at his judgment seat." Chrysostom says in hom. 37 in Matth., "After your day you will die; judgment and punishment follow; for in hell, the Psalmist says, who will praise you?" There, even if the word *immediately* were not added, still it is necessarily understood to be between the lines. Chrysostom refuted the error of those who thought Christ will preach after death and will lead the dead to penance.

But he uses this argument: After death judgment follows, and after judgment the punishment of hell, in hell no man can confess the Lord; thus, after death there is no place for penance. But if Chrysostom did not mean to say, the impious are judged immediately from death and are driven into hell but delayed all these things until the last day, his argument would be to no avail. For it would be answered in this middle time the dead can be preached, to provided the universal judgment is delayed. St. Augustine, in his work on the origin of the soul (lib. 2 cap. 4) says: "Now he most rightly and wholesomely believes that souls, after quitting the body are judged before they come to the final judgment to which they must submit when their bodies are restored to them."

To these we add the example of those who have witnessed that they were judged. St. Gregory writes (lib. 4 *Dialogorum*, cap. 36) on a certain Stephan, who, when he had died and was offered to judgment, heard the judge saying: "I did not command this one, but Stephan Ferrarius to be called," and so he came back to life while at the same time Stephan Ferrarius, who lived in a nearby place, died. St. Augustine relates a similar event in *de cura pro mortuis*, cap. 12, on a certain Curma. But Gregory adds that this did not take place by a true error, but that through it, as if it were an error, the one who had been dead and came back to life would relate torments and judgment to the living which remain for the impious after this life. In the same book, cap. 38, he relates the example on a certain Chrisorius, who, being placed at the point of death, while he was still living saw the sentence of his own damnation.

St. Bede relates to similar events (*hist.* lib. 5, cap. 14-15), about two men who died in the throes of despair because they had seen their judgment carried out and the sentence imposed. John Climacus relates a similar thing in his *Scala*, 7th step, about a certain hermit that, while on the point of death, heard as if he were placed in trial to answer accusations, and once was heard to say "It is false, I did not do it; I did it, but I did penance; you speak the truth and I have nothing to answer."

Next, a memorable example is extant in the life of St. Bruno, about a certain Parisian doctor, who in the very Church where the funeral rights were carried out, after his head was elevated on the bier, shouted: "By the just judgment of God I have been accused;" and on the following day, again shouted: "By the just judgment of God I have been judged"; and on the third day, "By the just judgment of God I have been damned". We must also note in regard to these examples, both the judgment of those which was carried out before death, and even more that of

Ch. V: The souls in Purgatory are certain of salvation 167

the Parisian which was delayed for three days after his death, pertain to a certain particular and extraordinary providence of God which he uses to build us up or to terrify us. Otherwise, normally it must be believed that judgment takes place immediately from death; for ordinarily the useful time of penance endures even to the last breath; as St. Leo clearly teaches in epistle 90 *ad Rusticum*. Nor is there a reason why after death judgment should be delayed, since God does not need witnesses nor allegations, but can judge in an instant. It could also be said, and perhaps more probably, in the examples related by Bede that judgment was not carried out before death, but merely foreshown, while in the example of the Parisian doctor, the judgment was not delayed to another day, but only manifested on another day.

It must also be observed that it cannot be defined for certain whether their judgment is delayed; whether they are judged on the spot after they relinquish the body; and similarly whether they are judged immediately by Christ in human form imposing sentence; or whether only by divine power, which is present everywhere, or whether the sentence is manifested by angels. What Scripture everywhere says is that Christ the man is the judge of the living and the dead, it understands on the *last general judgment*, for even before the incarnation a particular judgment was exercised. This is why it is not only not certain, but still not probable, what Innocent III affirms (*de contemptu mundi*, lib. 2, last chapter) that Christ will appear in the crucified form to the dying, both the good and the bad.

In regard to the *third*, that the sentence of judgment is hidden to souls when they are judged is false and impertinent. False because the particular judgment is made particularly for this purpose, so that the sentence would be made known to the one judged; for on account of others there will be a general judgment. Judgment is not necessary on account of God, for he knows all things, therefore it is only done to make it known to that soul who is judged, and the same is gathered from the visions cited above. But it is also impertinent since even if the sentence of the judge were not made known to them, still they could easily recognize *per se* what sort it is from the effect, because they will see themselves right away in hell, or in heaven, or in purgatory.

But someone will say they could doubt whether they were in hell or in purgatory. But it is not so, since in hell God is blasphemed, in purgatory he is praised; in hell there is no infused faith, nor any hope or charity, while in Purgatory all these things are found; therefore, the soul, which will see itself hope in God, praise and love God, clearly sees that it is not in hell.

But he could, they say, fear lest he might be sent into hell, although he was still not there, but this can also not be said: for here he believed according to the clearest testimonies of the Scriptures, after death it cannot happen that anyone from the good becomes wicked, or from the wicked becomes good, and none other than the wicked will be sent into hell. So when he sees that he loves God and hence is good, he will not fear damnation.

But someone will insist: Here we see that we love God, and still we are not certain whether we are just, so also those souls will not gather for certain their justice from their love.

Ch. V: The souls in Purgatory are certain of salvation

I respond: We do not see the infused habit of charity, whereby we are justified, but we gather from fallible conjectures that it is in us; but the souls separated from their bodies, just as they will clearly see themselves without dependence upon phantasms, so also they see all things which they have in themselves, and hence they see whether they have the true habit of charity or not; besides, they know the souls are immovable in good and in evil, therefore, even if they did not see their infused habit of charity, nevertheless they would know that they will never blaspheme God, nor have hatred for him, and hence are never going to be sent to hell. Then, from faith they know the souls of the impious are pushed into hell right after the death of the body, and their punishments are not delayed any further. All Catholics believe this from Luke 16:22, therefore the souls which see themselves outside of hell, believe firmly that they are never going to be sent into it.

In regard to *the fourth*, is utterly false that the souls are impeded from the recognition of their state by excessive torments, and hence think they are in hell and live in a certain disturbance and despair, as Luther says. Firstly, the soul of the rich man in hell, in Luke 16, was not impeded from the knowledge of his state; how much less, therefore, will the souls that are in Purgatory be impeded.

Secondly, that in this world men are impeded from right judgment by the intensity of sufferings, comes into being from wounding of the corporeal organ; but in purgatory the mind is pure, spiritual, and incorruptible.

Thirdly, because the Church says in the canon of the Mass: "Be mindful, O Lord, of your servants and handmaids, who preceded us with the sign of faith and sleep in the sleep of peace." There the Church prays for the souls of Purgatory, for it adds: "For these, O Lord, and all those resting in Christ we ask that you grant a place of refuge, light and peace." But certainly, those who are said to sleep in the sleep of peace, are not anxious, nor despair, but instead have a mixture with supreme tortures and incredible consolation on account of the certain hope of salvation.

Fourthly, because if they believed that they were damned, they would not pray for the living, nor would the say that they would be freed in short order if prayers were offered for them, as we see happened with St. Gregory (*dialog.* lib. 4, c. 40) and the other examples brought in the first question.

CHAPTER V
Objections Made from the Prayers of the Church are Answered

OME object, *firstly*, with certain testimonies of the Scriptures which the Church uses in the office of the dead. She desires to pray for souls that abide in Purgatory from Psalm 6:3, "My soul is exceedingly disturbed." And in the same place, verse 2: "Cleanse my soul, because my bones have been crushed." And Psalm 114 (115):3, "The sorrows of death surrounded me, and the dangers of hell found me." Certainly, things such as disturbance and anxiety cannot be born from punishments alone, but from uncertainty and fear of eternal damnation. If those souls were perfect in charity, and were certain of their salvation, they would not be so afraid, seeing that it is written: "The just man will not be sorrowful, whatever happens to him" (Proverbs 12:21).

I respond: It is foolish to understand what the Church uses from some Psalm in the office for the dead as being applied literally in all its parts to the dead; for how would we understand verses of the same Psalm 6:6 to be about the dead: "I will wash my bed every night, I will water my sheets with my tears"? Therefore, the Church usually reads the whole of some passage of Scripture on account of one or another teaching which bears on the present matter, even if the greater part of that passage does not bear on it. It is thus in the dedication of a Church, where the Gospel about Zacchaeus is read, only for the reason that the last words "Today salvation has entered this house", are suited in some mode to the dedication and consecration of a Church. In like manner, in the Assumption of the Blessed Virgin, the Church reads the Gospel of Martha and the Magdalene on account of these words: "Mary has chosen the best part, and it will not be taken from her." And so (that I might omit many others) in the office of the dead on account of the words, "Have mercy on me O Lord, because I am weak." (Psalm 6:2). And on account of that of Psalm 114 (115):9, "I will please the Lord in the land of the living." These whole psalms are read.

Additionally, what is assumed in the argument is also false, namely that disturbance and sadness are not born from suffering but from uncertainty or despair of salvation; for the Lord himself (John 12:27) says in his regard: "Now my soul is troubled," and in Matthew 26:37, he began to be sad and wept, and still neither uncertainty nor desperation could fall upon the Lord. But the passage of Proverbs ought not be received on any sadness you like, but on the sadness with dejection and despair, which causes death, which St. Paul calls the sadness of this age (2 Corinthians 7:10).

The second objection is taken from that prayer which is recited after the Gospel in the Mass for the dead: "O Lord, free the souls of all the faithful departed from the punishments of hell and from the deep lake; free them from the mouth of the lion lest the underworld would absorb them, lest they fall into obscurity, etc."

Some respond that the Church prays for those who are in agony so that they will not be damned to hell. But this is opposed to the part that says: "Free the souls of all the faithful departed", for they are not said to be in agony. Then, the use of the Church is that this prayer is said even on the anniversaries of the dead for those souls who had died many years ago. Others say this prayer is poured forth for those who are in hell, whom, it turns out, are freed later, as is related about Trajan. But that I might omit how improbable that history of Trajan is, those who are in hell have already fallen into obscurity and also were absorbed into the underworld. Therefore, what does the Church pray for when she asks that they not fall into darkness or be absorbed into the underworld? Next, the Church only prays for the faithful: "Free the souls of the faithful departed." But they are not faithful who are damned to hell.

Consequently, there are two other answers that can be given. One is that the Church prays for the souls of those who abide in Purgatory so that they will not be condemned to the eternal punishment of hell, though not because it is uncertain that they are not going to be damned to those punishments, but because God wants us to pray also for those things which we will receive for certain.

But one can object against this response that even if the Church sometimes prays for those things which it is not going to receive for certain, nevertheless, it does not pray for those things which it has already received; hence it has already received that these souls will not be damned since they have a certain sentence and are most secure. Next, the mind of the faithful, who pray for the dead, or desire they be prayed for, is certainly related by the fact that they help those souls and obtain for them relief from the present punishments of Purgatory.

But these objections are easily dealt with, for even if the souls of Purgatory had already received the first sentence in the particular judgment, and were freed from hell by that sentence, still the general judgment, wherein they are going to receive the second sentence, remains. In this regard, the Church, prays lest in the final judgment those souls would fall into obscurity or be absorbed into the underworld. It does not pray for that which the soul received but for that which it is going to receive.

Now, to that from the intention of the faithful, *I respond* that the intention would satisfy it, for in that prayer both things are asked, namely that the souls be freed from the punishments of hell, *i.e.* Purgatory, which are suffered at the present, and later that they would be freed from the sentence of damnation imposed in the last judgment.

There is another answer, that the Church truly prays insofar as to her intention, that souls be freed from the punishments of Purgatory, nevertheless she uses that mode of speaking as if the souls just left the body as if their eternal salvation were in danger, because it calls to mind and represents the day of deposition, or death, just like in the celebration of feasts of the Incarnation, Nativity, Apparition, of the Passion and Resurrection, and the Ascension of the Lord. There, the Church prays as if then Christ ought either to become incarnate or born, etc., because it represents these mysteries as present realities. Still, it does not intend to pray literally for this, say that the Word would become flesh, or born from a Virgin, etc., but so that the fruit of these mysteries would be applied to us; so also in the sacrifice for the dead, because the day of their death is commemorated, the Church so prays for them as if then they had died; and still intends to pray so that they would be freed from hell *in the mode in which they can be freed*; *i.e.*, that they would not be detained any longer in those punishments, or that some rest would be mixed with sorrows. Otherwise, how would it not be absurd that now after 1500 years to say for the Lord's arrival; "*Rorate caeli de super, et nubes pluant justum; aperiatur terra, et germinet Salvatorem,*"[11] and many other kinds of things; consequently, it is not absurd to say for the dead, "free them from the mouth of the lion, lest they fall into obscurity," etc.

---

[11] "Drop down dew, ye heavens, from above, and let the clouds rain the just: let the earth be opened, and bud forth a saviour." Isaiah 45:8

CHAPTER VI
On the Location of Purgatory

HE *fourth question* follows: Where is Purgatory? The Church has defined nothing on such a question, although there are many opinions.

1) *First,* is of those who think that souls are cleansed in the very spot where they had sinned, *i.e.* in different places. And indeed that souls are cleansed in different places is gathered probably enough from St. Gregory (*Dialog.* lib. 4, cap. 40 and cap. 55), who relates the soul of Paschasius and of a certain other man cleansed in bath houses. Also, from an epistle of Peter Damian about the miracles of his time, where he describes a vision on the purgation of the soul of S. Severinus in a certain river. But that all are punished in the place where they sinned is not probable, for as it happens, some sinned in many places, it does not have the appearance of truth that they will be cleansed in all of them. Besides, the aforesaid visions show the contrary; for Paschasius the deacon sinned at Rome in the election of a Pope, but was cleansed in the baths of Puteoli, and St. Severinus sinned in the palace of the Emperor, and was cleansed in a river.

2) *The second* opinion, is that the habitations of souls are not corporeal, as Augustine thought (lib. 12 *de Gen.* cap. 33), but he retracted it in *Retractions,* lib. 2 cap. 24.

3) *The third,* is that penal places for souls are this world, in which the souls remain in body as if in jail. Irenaeus relates and refutes this at the end of book 5, for

the Scripture says the souls after this life descend into hell, as is clear from Luke 16:22 and other places.

4) *The fourth*, hell, and the purgatory of the soul, is nothing apart from the accusing conscience punishing sins. So Philo in his book *de Congressu Quaerendae Eruditionis Gratiâ*, and Origen, as Jerome relates in epist. ad Avitum. This is refuted, for if this opinion were true we would be in hell or purgatory no less now than after our death.

5) *The fifth* opinion is that hell, and hence Purgatory (for they are neighboring places), are in the valley of Josaphat. Chrysostom relates that some fathers thought this (hom. *de praemiis beatorum*, tom. 3) and Gregory relates a similar opinion (lib. 4 *Dialog.* cap. 42). Perhaps their argument was that since Christ everywhere calls hell *Gehenna*, and Gehenna is a certain valley joined with the valley of Josaphat so that it seems to be a part of it; we will speak on that name below.

6) *The sixth* opinion is that hell is the state of the soul outside the body, for while it is in the body, it lives in the light, as is clear from its works; when it leaves the body, it can see no longer, unless it is blessed; and this is outward darkness. So Theophylactus relates on chapter 16 of Luke.

7) *The seventh* opinion is that it is a penal place of souls that is not earthly, but a foggy air where demons live. So Gregory of Nyssa thinks (*de Anima et resurrectione*) and Chrysostom (hom. *de praemiis beatorum*) as well as the author of the incomplete work on Matthew, hom. 53, whose opinion the history of St. Fursaeus favors that is found in Bede (*hist. Anglorum*, lib. 3, cap. 19), after he as died, when by Angels he is lead into heaven, they are shown the greatest fires above the air, which are preserved

(as the angel says), for the conflagration of the world, and there the works of men will be examined.

8) *The eighth* is the common teaching of the Scholastics, that Purgatory is within the bowels of the earth, near to hell. The Scholastics, in a common consensus, constitute that within the four corners of the earth, or one divided into four parts there is one place for the damned; another for those to be purged; a third for the infants dying without baptism; a fourth for the just who died before the passion of Christ which now remains empty. The sufficiency of these is altogether taken from the kinds of punishments; for there are all these penal places, every punishment is either only of loss, or of sense; and again either eternal or temporal. For punishment only of eternal loss, there is the limbo of children; for punishment only of temporal loss, there was the limbo of the Fathers; for the punishment of eternal loss and sense, there is hell; for the punishment of temporal loss and sense, there is Purgatory.

Yet, because Calvin says these are all fables (*Instit.* lib. 2, cap. 15, §9) and likewise his disciple Beza (in cap. 2 Act), and his teacher Bucer (in cap. 27 Matth.) each one of these must be proved. *First*, that within the bowels of the earth there is some place for souls that is called in the general vocabulary hell (*infernus*) we proved in book 4 *On Christ*, ch. 9, let the reader look there if he wishes to clearly see what pertains to that place.

Next, to the arguments which we then advanced, are added various eruptions of fire which appear in the earth, which St. Gregory does not rashly think are certain tokens of hell, existing within the bowels of the earth (lib. 4 *Dialog.* cap. 35), for in the same book, (cap. 30) he writes

Ch. VI: Where is Purgatory? 179

that he knew from a certain relation that at the same hour in which the Arian King Theodoric died, his soul was seen thrown into the pit of Vulcan, which is in Sicily. Laurence Surius, in his history for the year 1537, writes in regard to mount Hecla, a mountain on Iceland, from which flames break out and certain things are heard like terrible lightening, and souls often appear which say they are sent to that mountain. This is about hell in general.[12]

Now on the individual places. *First*, that the hell of the damned is in the deepest parts of the earth is proven; firstly, although that hell is within the bounds of the earth is already shown, still, in Luke 16:22 the soul of the rich man is said to have been in hell, and not only in hell, but even in the deepest place; seeing that he saw Lazarus, who then was also in subterranean places, again he ought to be facing him. Besides, reason itself demands that if the place of the blessed is in the highest heaven, the place of the damned would be in the place furthest from heaven, for nothing is more remote than the center of the earth.

Then, that Purgatory is also under the earth and near hell, is proven from those words of Acts 2:24: "After he loosed the sorrows of hell," which St. Augustine understood to be the punishments of Purgatory (epist. 99), "Free the souls of the dead from the punishments of hell and from the deep lake." *Secondly*, it is confirmed from the vision which Bede relates (lib. 5, cap. 13 *historiae*), where Purgatory was clearly seen touching upon the hell of the damned. Next, nearly all theologians teach that the

---

[12] Translator's note: While testimonies of this sort made an impression on men in the 16th century, today they are less impressive to most. Still, there is nothing to make such an explanation impossible.

damned and the souls of Purgatory are in the same place and tortured by the same fire.

Now, that the limbo of children is in hell is proved: the Council of Florence, in its last session, clearly defined that both those who are dead with mortal sin and those who with only original sin, descend right away into hell, still to be punished with different punishments; St. Augustine, in *de Baptismo parvulorum*, lib. 4, cap. 28 and *Hypognostici*, lib. 4, says that the Catholic faith knows none other than two places, the heaven of the blessed and the hell of the damned. Nevertheless, it is the common opinion of the Scholastics, that the limbo of children is in a place in hell higher than Purgatory, so that the fire does not touch them. Innocent III followed this opinion (cap. *Majores*, extra de Baptismo). But on this matter we will make a disputation in another place.

Lastly, the limbo of the Fathers is in hell, but in the highest part, and it is proved with sufficient accuracy in book 4 *de Christo*, cap. 10. We will repeat only one argument which in that place was treated too briefly. Therefore, 1 Kings 28:13, the soul of Samuel was seen to ascend from subterranean places: "I say," the witch says, "the gods ascend from the earth."

Our adversaries respond, that it was not truly Samuel but a devil in his form, as Tertullian teaches (*de anima*), as well as the author of the *Questions* cited by Justin Martyr (quaest. 52) and questions on the Old Testament (*quaest.* 27) cited by Augustine, and the author of the books on the miracles of Sacred Scripture, book 2 ch. 11, and Procopius and Eucherius on this passage of the book of kings, and Isidore, lib. 8 *etymologiar.* cap. 9, who is moved by these reasons.

Ch. VI: Where is Purgatory?

Firstly, it is not believable that Samuel was subject to a witch, or would have come of his own will, because that would confirm her magic art. *Secondly*, because Samuel would not suffer himself to be worshiped, as that shadow did. *Thirdly*, because he would not have said to Saul in verse 19: "Tomorrow you and your son will be with me." The soul of Saul was not going to the limbo of the Fathers, but to hell. *Fourthly*, because God denied the response to Saul through the prophets, through oracles and through dreams, as it is related in the chapter, therefore it is not believable that he would respond later through a witch.

But these not withstanding, it must be held that what appeared was truly the soul of Samuel and hence a forceful confirmation of our teaching on the subterranean location of Purgatory. In the first place, all the cited authors are either uncertain or unclear; but those who teach the contrary are certain and of renown, such as Josephus (*antiq.* lib. 6, cap. 15), Justin Martyr (*Dialog with Trypho*), Basil (*epist.* 80 *ad Eustachius the doctor*); Ambrose (in cap. 1 of Luke), Jerome (in cap. 8 of Isaiah), and Augustine (*de cura pro mortuis*, cap. 15). Nor is it opposed that Augustine (*ad Simplicianum*, lib. 2, quaest. 3) was uncertain whether that was the soul [of Samuel] or not, for he wrote later in his work *de cura pro mortuis* after he had considered the matter more diligently. Besides these fathers, more recent authors teach the same thing, such as Lyranus, Abulenis, Dennis the Carthusian and Cajetan.

There are also the strongest reasons for this teaching: 1) That Scripture perpetually calls what appeared "Samuel", in verse 12: "When the women saw Samuel;" and again in 15: "Samuel spoke to Saul," verse 14: "So Saul understood that it was Samuel." But certainly it would not have said that he understood it to be Samuel, but that he thought it was, if it were not really true.

2) Sirach 46:16-23 is placed in praise of Samuel because as a dead man he had prophesied and announced to the king what was about to come. But what praise is that which a devil of some species assumes and depicts? And this is an argument on account of what Augustine asserts in *de cura pro mortuis*, that truly it was Samuel that had appeared, whose testimony he had not recalled when he wrote to Simplicianus.

3) Because it foretold the future to Saul, which the devil cannot know, namely that he was going to die the next day with his sons, the army be destroyed and that David would rule after him, etc.

4) Lastly, because the contrary reasons conclude nothing.

So, I say to the *first*, Samuel did not come at the command of the witch, but at the command of God and he rather more impeded the magical art than confirmed it; for Samuel came before the spell would cause his arrival, and he ascended in a contrary mode to others who are roused by a spell, and the reason is because the witch was disturbed and said it was imposed on her. For if it is true, what the Rabbis write, that the shadows of the dead which are called upon by magical art, ascend upside down; but Samuel ascended standing upright, so that the head came first, then the breast, and lastly the feet were seen to emerge from the earth.

I say to the *second*, that adoration was not latria, but a reverence due to the soul of Samuel.

I say to the *third*, that "You will be with me," does not mean he would be in the bosom of Abraham, but under the earth, *i.e.* you will be dead, for although Jonathan was just among the sons of Saul, they were not going to descend to the same place, and still Samuel said in general: "You will be with me."

To the *fourth*, I say that God meant to show he was angry at Saul, and did this both by not responding when he was asked and by responding when he was not asked; for both are figures of anger. Add that when Saul asked God, if God would have responded, Saul could have turned away from war and punishment prepared for him by God; but when he asked the witch, all things were already prepared, the army drawn up and placed in his sight, so that he could not withdraw from battle by any means; therefore, then God, so that he might punish Saul more, foretold to him through his prophet the ruin of his sons and whole army.

Therefore, we have Purgatory, Hell, and the limbos of the fathers and children are locations under the earth.

CHAPTER VII
Whether after this Life, There is Some Place for Just Souls apart from Heaven and Purgatory

N the aforesaid subterranean receptacles for souls, theologians usually treat on two specific ones, which it is suitable to discuss here briefly for the purpose of treating the doctrine more fully. *Firstly*, they ask whether, apart from these places there might be some other place, where souls are retained before they arrive at the kingdom of heaven. *Secondly*, whether they can go out from these places.

In regard to the first, the difficulty is sufficiently great; because on the one hand, all theologians teach that there are no other receptacles apart from the four enumerated, and the Council of Florence defined in its last session that those having nothing to be purged are immediately received into heaven. On the other hand, Bede relates (*hist.* lib. 5, cap. 13) a very probable vision that he did not hesitate to trust. In it, it was shown to a certain soul which later returned to the body and said that apart from hell, purgatory and heaven, there a certain place like a most florid meadow, very bright, fragrant and pleasant, in which souls abided that suffered nothing but still remained there because they were not yet suitable for the beatific vision. Dennis the Carthusian adds many other things in conformity with that revelation in his dialog *de judicio particulari*, art. 31, and Louis Blosius in his *Monili Spirituali*, cap. 13.

It seems to me it must be said that it is not improbable that such a place is found and that it pertains to Purgatory; for even if there were no punishment of sense, still there is a punishment of loss; but punishment is not fitting except for a soul that has not yet been fully purged, and therefore it would be the mildest place of Purgatory, sort of like an aristocratic and honored prison.

Nevertheless, this must be added: the souls which tarry in that place not only lack beatitude, but are also afflicted and tortured by the delay of beatitude. Moreover, I said it seems to me that it is not *improbable* that such a place is found, because St. Thomas writes (4 dist. 21, quaest. 1, art.1) that in those matters in regard to purgatory that have not yet been determined by the Church, it favors those which are more in conformity to the aforesaid and the revelations of the Saints. The authority of Juan Torquemada also moves me, seeing that he was a most learned man and one of the best Cardinals, who in the prologue which is prefaced to the Revelations of St. Brigit, he eagerly expended much energy on these revelations and did not hesitate to affirm that it is fitting for St. Brigit what is said in Judith 8:28, "All the things which you spoke are true, and there is no fault in your speech." St. Brigit writes (lib. 4 cap. 124) about a certain soul in Purgatory that had no other punishment but the sorrow from the longing for that happiness, so long delayed.

CHAPTER VIII
Whether Souls of the Dead might Avail to Leave their Receptacles

HE other question can have a threefold sense. *First*, whether souls that go out can never return because they are transferred from one receptacle to another; *second*, whether they can go out so that they might again return to their place; *third*, whether they can go out in such a way that they might live here again with us.

As far as the first sense, it is easy to respond: From the hell of the damned and the limbo of children one cannot go out again; from Purgatory and the limbo of the Fathers it is granted, for there are souls of the impious condemned to perpetual prisons and the fires of hell, and likewise the souls of children to perpetual exile and darkness. But the souls of the Holy Fathers were condemned to a temporal exile, and the souls of Purgatory to temporal prisons. The reason is the cause of the prison, or exile of the damned is actual mortal sin, or original sin, which is never remitted; the cause of the exile of the Fathers was temporal debt contracted from the sin of the first parents; by that sin heaven was closed, and it could not be opened except by the real shedding of the blood of Christ; but the cause of Purgatory is to undergo temporal punishment which necessarily has an end.

Nevertheless, the authority of John Damascene is against this, who, in an oration on the dead, says that by the prayers of St. Thecla the soul of Falconilla, a certain

Ch. VIII: Do the dead leave their places? 187

pagan woman, was delivered from hell, and by the prayers of St. Pope Gregory the Great the soul of Trajan was delivered from hell.

I respond: If these histories have to be defended, it would be fitting to say that Trajan was not absolutely damned to hell, but only punished in hell *according to his present demerits, and his sentence suspended on account of the foreseen prayers of St. Gregory*; and besides, he did not pass immediately from hell to heaven, but first united to the body, and then baptized, and did penance in this life; for this is the common answer of St. Thomas, Durandus, Richardus, and of others (in 4 dist. 45). Nevertheless, there is no witness that relates Trajan's resurrection, nor does any ancient writer call it to mind, and it is opposed to the teaching of Damascene, who clearly enough teaches that Trajan passed from hell to heaven, but not that he returned to this life, and if he did penance he did it in hell; nevertheless, the cited authors only rest upon the authority of Damascene. Therefore, I propose in its place the teaching of Melchior Cano, who altogether disproves this history as made up (*de locis*, lib. 11 cap. 2), and Domingo de Soto who in 4 dist. 45, quaest. 2 art. 2, says this history was very hard for him to trust, not withstanding the defense by Alonso Chacón, published three years ago. But the reasons, whereby I am moved, are four.

1) *First*, because whoever admits this history, they do it on account of the authority of Damascene, but that book is not of Damascene and it can easily be shown, for in that book the authority not only says Trajan and Falconilla passed from hell to heaven, but also that many others who had descended into hell because they lacked divine faith, were converted by Christ and saved when he descended to

hell, which is erroneous in itself and contrary to the words of Damascene, (*de fide*, lib. 2, cap. 4) where he says that death is to men what the fall was to angels.

2) *The second* reason is that no Latin authority mentions this history, such as Paul the Deacon, Anasthasius the Librarian, Marians Scotus, Ado, and not even Bede himself, who was very devoted to St. Gregory, and not even in the Roman Church itself and its archives, since there exists no mention of this event. When John the Deacon wrote the life of St Gregory, he most diligently gathered records from the Roman archives, and still (lib. 2 cap. 44), he says this history on Trajan was found in a certain English Church; the Romans did not put certain faith in it.

3) *Third*, because St. Gregory (lib. 34, *Mor.*, cap. 13 et 16) clearly teaches that one cannot pray for dead unbelievers, and in the same way, not for the devil, seeing that they are in the same eternal and irrevocable damnation. So how is it believable that he did this? Abulensis responds (quaest. 57 and in 4 Kings) that Gregory sinned mortally in praying for Trajan. This is absolutely absurd and truly blasphemous, since it is a fact that Gregory was not only a holy man but also very prudent. Next, if he sinned mortally in so praying, how was it that he was heard? Is God pleased when he is offended? Chacón answers that Gregory did not sin in so praying, but rather merited the effect, even though normally it is not permitted to pray for the damned, still it is permitted from a peculiar divine instinct.

Against this, the same history relates that Gregory, on account of this sin, was punished with perpetual stomach and foot pain. He responds that this suffering was not

Ch. VIII: Do the dead leave their places?   189

given to Gregory as a penalty, but lest glorification would creep up on him; but against this, Peter the deacon, whom he cites from a certain book in the Vatican Library, says that Gregory was told by an angel that because he presumed to ask for this, he would labor even to death in pain, etc., therefore he was punished for sin, since presumption is a sin.

4) *The fourth* reason is that the arguments of Chacón do not conclude the matter; he rests especially upon these witnesses. *Firstly*, the testimony of Peter and John, the deacons of Gregory, which he says are extant in the Vatican library. *Secondly*, on the testimony of an unnamed author, who wrote the life of St. Gregory that is prefaced to his works printed at Basel in 1564. The author seems to have been someone that lived in the time of Gregory himself. *Thirdly*, on the testimony of Damascene. *Fourthly*, on the testimony of John the Deacon (lib. 2 cap. 44) on the life of St. Gregory. *Fifthly*, on the testimony of St. Thomas. *Sixthly*, on the testimony of St. Brigit. *Seventhly*, on the testimony of Mechtilidis.

The first testimony seems suspect to me; for if it were truly of Peter the Deacon, John the deacon would not have said this history is not extant in the Roman Church, but only among the English. *Besides*, this Peter says that Gregory sought from God that whoever was buried in the Church of St. Andrea on the Scaurus hill can not be damned, provided they held Christian faith. But certainly Gregory, a very prudent man, would never have prayed in this way, for he either understands informed faith or formed faith; first, if informed, then he meant dying men are saved without charity; but who would believe that? If formed, it was not necessary that they perish, for wherever they are buried who die with charity, they cannot be damned. Add that the whole fragment is redolent with novelty and thus seems suspicious; for it calls Gregory *divus*, a name that was not used at that time. Likewise, it places Cardinals ahead of bishops, which is opposed to John the Deacon's usage, who in the life of St. Gregory writes that many from among the Cardinals were usually promoted to the Episcopate by Gregory, as though to a higher degree. It also has several other signs of novelty.

The second testimony advances nothing new; but the author, without a name, did not live in the time of St. Gregory, rather in a later time. For he reduced into a compendium life of St. Gregory what John the deacon had written more profusely.

The third testimony has already been rejected.

The fourth testimony is against Chacón himself, for John the Deacon says the soul of Trajan was not freed from hell but only that it was obtained for him that he would not suffer the punishment of fire in hell; Chacón, however, would have it that he is among the blessed in heaven.

The fifth testimony is also against him, since St. Thomas, where he avowedly treats this, namely in 4, dist. 45, quaest. 2, thinks it very probable that the soul of Trajan was only freed from the punishments of hell even to the day of judgment, and thereafter, is going to be tortured with the rest.

The sixth is expressly against it, for Mechtildis says he asked from the Lord what he would do with the souls of Samson, Solomon, Origen and Trajan, and God answered that he meant for it to be unknown to all what he did from his generosity. So, if God wanted it to be unknown, then one must not put any trust in the authors that say Trajan

Ch. VIII: Do the dead leave their places?

is in heaven. Add that God, in this revelation, joins Trajan with Origen; but in the spiritual meadow cited by the seventh Council as well as by John the deacon in his life of St. Gregory (lib. 2 cap. 45), another revelation is related in which Origen was seen in the fires of hell with Arius and Nestorius, and in the fifth Council, cap. 11, it says anathema to Origen just as to Arius, Nestorius and other heretics.

In regard now to the second question, certain men think the souls cannot ever go out from their receptacles and all apparitions are of demons who pretend to be souls going out from Purgatory and asking for assistance. So thought Tertullian (*de anima*), and the author of questions to Antioch, quaest. 11 and 13. Chrysostom appears to say the same thing (homil. 29 in Matth. and hom. 1 & 4 on Lazarus) as well as Theophylactus in cap. 8 Matth. Although these two, if they are read correctly, do not say that souls can not go out to us in any manner, but simply not of their own will; nor do they become demons, nor wander among us after the fashion of demons. The heretics of this time mock all apparitions of souls as illusions of demons, especially the Centuriators.

Nevertheless, St. Augustine's teaching is the truest (*de cura pro mortuis*, cap. 15-16), that it is of the greatest impudence to deny that souls return to us either at God's command or with his permission; for we have the testimony of very serious authors on the return of souls from all receptacles, apart from the limbo of children. That the souls of the blessed in heaven should come to us at some point is certain from examples cited by Eusebius (*histor.* lib. 6, cap. 5), Augustine (*de cura pro mortuis*, cap. 16) Sulpitius, in the life of Martin, Paulinus, in the life of

Ambrose, Theodoret (lib. 5, hist. cap. 24), Gregory (lib. 3 Dialog. cap. 24 & 25) and in the seventh Council, act 4.

That souls appeared from the limbo of the Fathers, St. Augustine proves (*loc. cit.*) from 1 Kings 1:28, where the soul of Samuel appeared to Saul, and in Matthew 17 where Moses appeared with Elijah on mount Thabor. Although Hilary and Ambrose say on this passage that Moses still lives, nevertheless the contrary is expressly contained in Deuteronomy 34:5 and Joshua 1:1-2.

That souls have appeared from Purgatory, there are examples cited by Gregory (*Dialog.* lib. 4, capl 40 & 55) and other authors whom we cited above. Then from hell, the author of the books on the properties of bees relates many examples, and the same appear from that apparition of the Parisian Doctor in the life of St. Bruno, who, three days after his death, said that he was condemned. It is believable that a soul descended right away into hell, but still appeared and in the first place manifested its accusation; secondly its judgment; thirdly its damnation, so that it would be known to many by way of example.

In regard to the third part of the question, that some from Purgatory or the limbo of the Fathers were recalled to life, there cannot be a doubt for anyone. For the those whom Elijah, Elisha and our Lord Jesus Christ raised from the dead, as well as those raised by Peter and Paul when they were faithful, are believed to have been in Purgatory or in limbo; nor does anything unseemly follow, if from these places some rose again, accordingly, this is nothing other than to change exile, or prison for them.

But someone will object: They were certain of their salvation, and by resurrection they become uncertain. Abulensis responds well (q. 57 in 4 Regum), that all of those who are recalled to life from Purgatory or the limbo of the Fathers were, without a doubt, confirmed in grace so that in no way could they perish because otherwise it would be an injury for them.

Moreover, that from heaven or the hell of the damned they could be recalled to life seems unbelievable, unless there were examples that could not be denied. Now, St. Gregory writes about St. Fortunatus raising Marcellus, a certain holy man (*Dialog*. lib. 1 c. 9), who had been lead by the Angels into the best place, and in chapter 12 he writes about St. Severus who raised a certain very wicked man that had been lead down by demons into hell. Egesippus writes (lib. 3 c. 2) that St. Peter raised a certain relation of Caesar, a heathen, from death. Nor can there be any doubt that the Apostles raised some pagans. Maximus (serm. 2 de S. Agnete) says that St. Agnete raised the son of a Prefect that had died in mortal sin. And Evodius (lib. 1 de miraculis S. Stephani), says that a child dead before baptism was brought to life by the relics of St. Stephen.

Therefore, I say those presently blessed cannot be recalled to life. Beatitude includes a certitude about not losing any happiness, as St. Augustine teaches (*de corrept. et gratia*, cap. 10), and the reason is clear, because beatitude is the state perfected by the joining of all goods; but someone who does not have certitude does not have all goods. Therefore, if some holy men are returned to the body, they were not blessed, but God, foreseeing their being raised, delayed their beatification and meanwhile detained them in some very good place, as happened to Marcellus, about whom Gregory speaks.

I will say the same thing about the damned. Someone that has been damned absolutely to eternal punishments cannot be recalled to life because otherwise, the damnation of the impious would be uncertain. St. Augustine correctly says that it is of great presumption to assert they are not going to remain perpetually in fire, to whom Truth says: "Go into the eternal fire;" but Truth says this to all whom it damns, both in the particular and in the universal judgment. *Besides*, there would be none of the damned who could hope for salvation and for whom we could not pray; but now we do not pray for damned infidels, because according to faith we believe they cannot be saved; but if they can at least be saved by privilege, certainly, we must pray for them just as in this world we pray for those who are obstinate in evil that God would grant to them efficacious grace, which certainly is not given except by a privilege.

But Abulenis objects in question 57, on the 4th book of Kings: For someone raised from the hell of the damned, neither sin nor punishment is remitted by the same raising, nor is there another miracle required here than a simple raising from the dead, rather an equivalent benefit is given, because he is placed in a state in which he will be able to be free from sin and punishment, from which all the aforesaid absurdities follow, which will not be certain for the impious in damnation; but if they could hope for them, it would be lawful to pray for them.

To these examples, which are advanced, de Soto responds (4 dist. 45, quaest. 2 art. 2) that all the heathen whom the Apostle raised labored in invincible ignorance of the faith, and hence were in Purgatory.

But what will de Soto answer to St. Ambrose (serm. 90) and to St. Maximus (in serm. 2), who say that St. Agnetis raised the son of the prefect, whom the devil had slain since he meant to deflower the holy maiden? I say they who are raised, when they merit eternal punishments, were not damned rather their judgment was suspended and in the mean time they were punished according to the present injustice, as St. Thomas teaches in 4 sent. dist. 45, q. 92, art. 2, just as Richardus, Durandus and others explain the same thing.

CHAPTER IX
On the Time in which Purgatory Endures

NOW on the time in which Purgatory will remain, there are two extreme errors. The first error is that of Origen, who extended the times of Purgatory beyond the day of the resurrection, so that he has in homily 14 in Luke: "I think that even after the resurrection from the dead we need the sacrament to wash and cleanse us, for no man can rise again with filth." Nevertheless, this error has been explored, for St. Augustine (lib. 21 *de civitate Dei*, cap. 16) says: "We suppose that there will be no Purgatorial punishments except before that last and tremendous judgment." And the reason is, because the Lord says that in the judgment there will be only two ranks of men, one of the blessed, the other of the damned (Matth. 25).

But someone will say: The soul alone did not sin, but once with the body, therefore it should be purged then with the body, hence, after the resurrection men will be purged. *I respond:* if that would conclude the argument, it would also prove that the soul cannot be separated to be punished in hell, nor enjoy the delights of heaven, which is against the Gospel, "I am tortured in this flame" (Luke 16:24), and "Today you will be with me in paradise" (Luke 23:43).

Therefore, I say the soul is duly punished even by itself, because it is the subject and efficient cause of sin; for there are certain human acts which cannot be done except from the whole composite, nor received except in the whole composite, such as all those which are done by organic potencies, *e.g.* to speak, see, hear, etc., and such things, after the dissolution of the composite, are no longer found. And if indeed such were a sin, it would clearly conclude the argument. But it is not so, for sin is an act of free will, and therefore properly said to come into being by the will alone and found formally in the will alone. Consequently, after the dissolution of man, the whole sin is only found in the will, and by that fact, in the soul, but not in dead flesh; moreover, it ought to be punished or purged in that place where it is found.

Add also, that the flesh is punished in its mode; for as the separated soul is punished with the penalty of loss, because it lacks the vision of God, and the punishment of sense, because it is tortured in fire, so the flesh is punished by the fire of loss, because it lacks life and the punishment of sense, although improperly, because it rots little by little and is reduced to ash; nevertheless, the first answer is better, for even the bodies of the saints that do not need purgation suffer this.

The second error is of Luther, who on the contrary makes Purgatory too short. He would have it that anyone who dies in faith has the remainder of his sins purged by the sorrow of death, and so there is no further Purgatory than death itself. This error can be easily refuted. By the remaining sins, either the *fomes*[13] are understood, or bad habits that were contracted, or the undergoing of temporal punishments and venial sins. These alone, and all others can remain in a man that has been justified, which pertain

---

[13] *Translator's note: The fomes* is a technical term from *fomes peccati*, meaning literally "tinder for sin" and refers to concupiscence.

to sin and hence can be said to be the remainder of one's sins. First, the *fomes* is certainly abolished in death, because then sensuality is extinguished, but we do not constitute Purgatory due to the *fomes*, otherwise even baptized infants that die would need to suffer the punishments of Purgatory, since Baptism does not wash away the *fomes*. But Augustine, in the cited passage of *City of God*, teaches precisely that children of this sort do not suffer any purgatorial punishments. Now in regard to bad habits, those which exist in the will are not necessarily extinguished by death, seeing that they are in the powers that are not bound to an organ. Nevertheless, on account of habits of this sort we constitute Purgatory since otherwise it would follow that adults who are baptized after they have contracted bad habits, and immediately die, or certainly are killed for Christ, could not be saved except by Purgatory because neither Baptism nor Martyrdom dissolves habits of this kind. We see the baptized still have these same wicked inclinations which they had before, and it is necessary for them to abolish habits of this sort little by little with contrary acts.

Therefore, it is believable that all these habits are abolished by the first contrary act of the separated soul, which it elicits immediately from the separation. For, even if this habit, contracted in one act, cannot be destroyed by many acts nevertheless, there it will be able to be because that act will be much more forceful, seeing that then the soul will be more powerful in regard to spiritual acts and it will not have the contrary *fomites* and resistance as it has here.

Thus, it remains to speak of suffering punishment and venial sin, which can properly be called the remainder of

Ch. IX: How long is Purgatory?

sin, which is the reason why Purgatory exists. Moreover, it is certain that sometimes these remnants are purged in death, and at other times it is certain they are not, whereas, at other times there is a doubt as to whether this happened and it is very probable that it was partly purged and partly not.

I will prove these individually. For the first, a violent death received for Christ, which is called martyrdom, without a doubt cleanses all remnants of this sort. Cyprian clearly says that all sins are cleansed in passion (lib. 4 epist. 2); that he is not speaking about mortal sins is obvious because in the same place he says that without charity martyrdom is of no benefit whatsoever. St. Paul taught this before Cyprian in 1 Cor. 13. Therefore, the Church never prays for martyrs, because, as St. Augustine says on the words of the Apostle: "It is an injury to pray for a martyr, to whose prayers we ought to be commended."

I prove the second: Those who die against their will or without the use of reason, such as the insane, those who die in their sleep and those who die instantly cannot be purged by that death in any mode; for either death itself absolutely purges, or by reason of some voluntary concomitant act itself. Not the former because death is, according to what it is, natural, at least after the sin of our first parents. This is why it is common to both the good and the bad, nay more to men and beasts; but by natural things which necessarily must come about we do not merit or lose merit, nor can we dissolve debts contracted voluntarily, so if death purges, it happens by reason of a voluntary concomitant act. But we are speaking in this place about those men who die without any act of this sort. Besides, we often see the best men suffer a very hard death, and those that are not good suffer a very light one. But if in death the remnants of sin should be purged, then necessarily the contrary ought to happen.

I prove the third: There are many who bear death with equanimity, whose patience without a doubt helps to make satisfaction, but whether those sufferings are equivalent to the debts contracted from sin, nobody can know for certain.

Apart from these errors there was an opinion of Domingo de Soto that no one in Purgatory remains beyond ten years (4 Sent. dist. 19 quaest. 3, art. 2). His reasoning is that if here on earth we can be freed from all punishments in a short time by certain punishments, why not more quickly in Purgatory since those punishments are infinitely more serious punishments and more intense than the former? Besides, here punishments are extended because they cannot be very intense or they would destroy the subject; but after this life they can be as intense as possible, because the subject is incorruptible. Thus, it is believable that God purges those souls gasping for glory in the shortest time by the most intense punishments. But these reasons do not conclude the matter.

To the first it can be said that here is the time of mercy and there is the time of justice.

To the second I say, God can compensate extension with intension, but he refuses; otherwise it would follow that souls do not remain in Purgatory for one hour, because God can, by increasing the intensity, redirect the punishments of ten years to one hour.

Besides, his opinion is opposed to approved visions of the Saints. Bede writes that the punishments of Purgatory were shown to a certain man, and it was said to him that souls which abide in Purgatory are all going to be saved on the day of judgment, although some will be assisted with prayers and almsgiving of the living, and above all the sacrifice of the altar, so that they will be freed even before the day of judgment (lib. 5 hist. cap. 13). There, he clearly shows some men that already died will remain in Purgatory even to the day of judgment. We can advance many similar visions from Dennis the Carthusian and others.

The custom of the Church is also opposed to this opinion, which celebrates an anniversary Mass for the dead, even if it is certain they died a hundred or two-hundred years ago. Certainly the Church would not do that if she believed that souls are not punished beyond ten years. Consequently, the matter is still uncertain and cannot be defined without temerity.

CHAPTER X
What Kind of Punishment is in Purgatory?

N the punishment of Purgatory there are some things that are certain and some that are in doubt. *Firstly*, it is certain that the punishment of Purgatory is not despair and fear of hell, as Luther's thinking which has already been refuted.

Secondly, it is also certain that one of the punishments of Purgatory is the loss of the divine vision; souls cannot not suffer since they see they are impeded from the enjoyment of the supreme good on account of their faults; this is called the punishment of loss [*pœna damni*].

Thirdly, it is certain that apart from this punishment there is also another punishment which theologians call the punishment of sense [*pœna sensus*], which consists in some sorrow arising from something other than the loss of the vision of God. One who sins turns himself away from the supreme good and turns inordinately to creatures, so later he ought to be punished not only with the loss of the supreme good, but even affliction inflicted by another created object.

Fourthly, it is certain that in Purgatory, just as also in hell, there is the punishment of fire, whether this fire is received properly or metaphorically, and whether it means the punishment of sense or of loss, as some men would have it. That there is some fire in Purgatory and hell is obvious both from the words of St. Paul "He will be saved as if by fire" (1 Cor. 3:15), and Matthew 25:41, "Go into the eternal fire," and from the testimonies of the Fathers cited in book 1, for all call the punishment of Purgatory fire.

With these being posited for certain, and all agreeing on them, there is a doubt: 1) Whether that fire is a fire properly so-called, or metaphorically? 2) If it is properly so-called, how could it affect disembodied spirits? 3) By whom are these punishments administered, by demons, angels, or do they happen themselves? 4) Whether these punishments are greater than the punishments of this life?

CHAPTER XI
The Fire of Purgatory is Corporeal

N regard to the *first*, the common opinion of theologians is that it is a true and proper fire and of the same species with our element. Such an opinion is indeed not *de fide*, because it has never been defined by the Church; nay more, in the Council of Florence the Greeks professed that they do not posit a fire in Purgatory, and still in the last session a definition was made in which Purgatory was defined but with no mention of fire. Still, it is a very probable opinion.

Firstly, on account of the consensus of the Scholastics, who cannot be scorned except with temerity.

Secondly, on account of the authority of Gregory (*Dialogorum*, lib. 4 cap. 29) where he carefully asserts that the fire, in which souls are punished, is corporeal. Nor is it opposed that in book 15, cap. 14 of the *Morals* he says the fire of hell is incorporeal, since it is a mistake of copyists, who placed *incorporeum* for *corporeum*, as is clear from what follows, since he says it burns corporally.

Thirdly, on account of Augustine, who inclined to the same opinion (*de civitate Dei*, lib. 21 cap. 10).

Fourthly, because in Scripture everywhere punishment of the impious is called fire, and the rule of theologians is that the words of Scripture are received properly when nothing absurd follows.

Fifthly, because the bodies of the damned will be punished with fire after the resurrection, as is clear in Matthew 25:41, "Go into the eternal fire," but bodies cannot be burned except by a corporeal fire. Further, the fire for the bodies of the damned is the same as for disembodied spirits, for it is said: "which was prepared for the devil and his angels."

Sixthly, because in Wisdom 11:17, it is says, that the very things whereby a man sinned will torture him, but men often sin by desiring objects of sensible delight, therefore they are often punished by sensible objects; so the fire, whereby they are punished, is sensible.

Seventhly, it is confirmed from eruptions of fire on mount Aetna, and other places about which we spoke in chapter 6.

CHAPTER XII
It Cannot be Known how Corporeal Fire Burns Souls

N the *second* doubt, the truest opinion is that it cannot be known in this life how a corporeal fire acts on the incorporeal soul; for Durandus nobly confesses (4 dist. 44 quaest. ult), and before him St. Augustine (*City of God*, lib. 21, cap. 10) that souls are tortured by a marvelous fire, but in true modes; and St. Gregory (lib. 4 *Dialog.* cap. 29) says that souls undergo invisible punishment from a visible fire in ways that are secret and unknown to us. But although we do not know how it happens, still, it can be so, as Augustine teaches from a similitude: We see the incorporeal soul united to the human body and give it life, and rejoices with it although the mode of this union is plainly ineffable. Who grasps how the spirit is the form of the body, when between body and soul there is no proportion? Therefore, just as a spirit can be united to the flesh to communicate life to it, so also can a spirit be united to fire for it to undergo punishment from it, although the mode of each union is properly unknown.

CHAPTER XIII
Whether Souls in Purgatory are Tortured by Demons

N the third uncertainty, the matter is altogether unclear; for the Scholastics, such as St. Thomas, teach they are neither tortured by demons or angels, but the fire alone (4 dist. 20 art. 5) and they give the reason that all the souls of Purgatory conquered the devil in their last conflict, so it is not fitting for divine justice to permit them to be troubled by the enemy they overthrew. *Next*, here on earth the demons trouble the perfect, because they hope that they can cause them to sin; but they know that the souls of Purgatory are confirmed in grace, cannot yield and that vexation will hasten them to purgation sooner; so it is not believable that the souls are tortured by an act of the demons.

On the other hand, many revelations teach that the souls of Purgatory are tortured by demons, such as that of Blessed Fursaeus, cited by Bede (*hist.* lib. 3, c. 19) and Dennis the Carthusian in his work on the last things, not to mention in book 1 of the life of St. Bernard, ch. 12. Therefore, this remains among the secrets that will be made clear to us in its time.

CHAPTER XIV
On the Gravity of Punishments

N the fourth, the punishments of Purgatory are very severe, and no punishments of this life can be compared with these, as the Fathers constantly teach. Augustine says, commenting on Psalm 37 (38): "Although he will be saved by fire, still that fire will be more severe than whatever a man can suffer in this life." St. Gregory says, commenting on Psalm 3: "That transitory fire I think more unbearable than every tribulation of the present life." St. Bede, commenting on the same Psalm, says that no punishments of martyrs or thieves can be compared with those purgatorial punishments. St. Anselm holds the same thing (commenting on 1 Cor. 3) and St. Bernard in his sermon *on the death of Humbert*.

All revelations which Bede cites (*Histor.* lib. 3 & 5) prove the same thing, as well as those cited by St. Brigit and Dennis the Carthusian and what is contained in the life of the miraculous Christina.

Reason proves the same thing, at least in regard to the *poena sensus*. Three things coincide with both sorrow and joy; potency, object and the union of one thing with another. Now, in regard to potency, without comparison the rational potency has more capacity for sorrow than the animal; in regard to apprehension, the intellect is like a font, sense like a small brook; in regard to the appetite, the will is like the font, the lower appetite is like a brook. Therefore, when the naked soul is tortured the greatest

Ch. XIV: The gravity of the punishments

suffering it ought to be on the side of the one suffering; in this life it is not only the soul but also the body that is tortured and through the body some of the suffering is also transferred to the soul.

In regard to the object, if it is a true fire there, it will be altogether the most bitter, since it was only established for this purpose, that it would be an instrument of divine justice; if it is not a true fire, it will be something much more horrible, such that God could prepare, which he willed to show his power.

Inasmuch as it regards the union, it will be the greatest; here, where everything is corporal, there is no union except through contact with the extremities, and superficial; but there punishment will penetrate the soul itself.

However, all admit in some mode that the punishments of Purgatory are greater than those of this life, nevertheless, there is a doubt how this is understood. St. Thomas teaches two things in 4 dist. 30 quaest. 1, art. 2. 1) The *poena damni* is the greatest of punishments which can be found in Purgatory and in this life; 2) He says the least punishment of Purgatory is greater than the greatest punishment of this life.

He proves the first because, just as possession of a desired good begets joy, so the absence of a desired good begets sorrow. But the good which the souls of Purgatory long for is the supreme good and the desire is thus the greatest; for the intellect more clearly recognizes how great a good it is to see God and the appetite, and the strength of the appetite, as well as infused charity, will go out and is the most intense, nor is it impeded by a corporeal mass and sensible delectations. In this life examples can be given, say if someone were disturbed by a vehement hunger, or would burn with an unbearable thirst, and see before him a table laden with the best food and sweetest wine, but cannot touch anything, and still he would know all these things were otherwise prepared for himself.

Next, St. Thomas proves the second, because everyone who abides in purgatory is tortured at least by this *poena damni*, which is the greatest of all, therefore the least punishment of Purgatory is greater than the greatest punishment of this life.

But St. Bonaventure (in 4 dist. 20 art. 1 q. 2) teaches *firstly*, the punishment of loss in Purgatory is not greater than every punishment, whether of Purgatory or of this life. *Secondly*, he teaches that the punishments of purgatory are greater than the punishments of this life, only in this sense, because the greatest punishment of Purgatory is greater than the greatest punishment of this life, although some punishment of purgatory is found lesser than some punishment of this life. I find this opinion more pleasing. Although the absence of the supreme good of itself would beget supreme sorrow in the lover, nevertheless, in Purgatory this sadness is mitigated and lifted in a great degree on account of a certain hope of acquiring that good; for that certain hope brings an incredible joy and from there, the closer it comes to the end of that exile, the more joy increases. Therefore, only in hell is the *poena damni* the greatest, because it is connected to certain desperation. Chrysostom speaks about this (hom. 24 in Matth) when he says a thousand hells are nothing if they are conferred with the loss of the divine sight, and Augustine, who in *Enchirid.* cap. 112, says the least *poena*

Ch. XIV: The gravity of the punishments

damni, if it is eternal, is greater than all the punishments of this life.

Someone might say: But the damned do not love God, thus, they do not desire to see him. *I respond:* They do not love God on account of God, but still, *on account of themselves* they are compelled to ardently desire his sight because they understand their supreme good is constituted in the vision of God.

This argument is confirmed, *firstly*, because if the *poena damni* were the most terrible, even in Purgatory, it would follow that the Fathers in limbo suffered the most terrible punishment; but this is completely false, as we see in Luke 16:25 where Abraham says to the rich man about Lazarus: "You are tortured, but he is consoled." And St. Augustine (epist. 99) denies that of Acts 2:24 can be understood about the Holy Fathers, "After the sorrows of hell were loosed," because Christ found them not in exceeding suffering, but in rest. And St. Gregory (*Moral.* lib. 13, cap. 22), says the Fathers in hell had no torment, but rest.

It is confirmed *secondly* because Augustine, Gregory, Bede, Anselm, and Bernard, although they say the punishment of Purgatory is greater than every punishment of this life, they clearly speak about the punishment *of fire*, through which every punishment of *sense* is understood, not of loss.

Then, what was said by Bonaventure is proven *firstly*, because from certain revelations it is clear that the punishment of some men is so scanty that they seem to suffer nothing, such as those who are clothed in white vestments that were seen in pleasant and lucid places, cited by Bede (lib. 5 *hist.* c. 13).

What Bonaventure says is proved *secondly*, because it can happen that someone tarries there bearing no debt with himself but one idle word; it seems absurd that on account of only one idle word someone ought to suffer graver punishments than all those of this life.

Thirdly, although there is the question as to whether the punishment of purgatory will always torture in an equally grave manner from the beginning even to the end of purgation, or whether it is diminished little by little until the end comes, still, the opinion is more probable that it is remitted little by little. Hence it follows that not every punishment of Purgatory is greater than the greatest punishment of this life, for that punishment of Purgatory which is near the end ought to be nearly remitted, so that it can no longer be remitted, but here very intense punishments are found that could remit a great many.

Now we prove that the punishment of Purgatory is incrementally remitted: St. Bernard, in the life of St. Malachi, writes that while Malachi was praying for his dead sister, she appeared to him three times. 1) in a black garment and outside of a Church; 2) in a gray garment and standing at the threshold of a Church; 3) in a white garment and at the altar itself with the rest of the saints. From such he understood that the soul of his sister was little by little being remitted of its punishments as it came to the end of its purgation. Many similar visions could be advanced.

CHAPTER XV
The Suffrage of the Church Benefits the Dead

E are going to explain four things in regard to the suffrage for the dead. *First*, whether the suffrage of the living benefits the dead; *second*, how many kinds of suffrage there are; *third*, by whom it can be made; *fourth*, whom they benefit.

First, all the heretics of this time as well as other older ones whom we cited in the beginning of this disputation, deny that suffrage of the living benefits the dead. Moreover, that it does benefit can be proven from the Scriptures, the Councils, the Fathers and apparitions of souls, all of which ought to be sought from the first question. To these, reason must be added, which then we did not advance, because it presupposes that Purgatory exists, but at that time we had not yet shown it.

The reasoning is of Peter the Cluniac (*contra Petrobusianos*): The whole Church is one body, the head is Christ; therefore it ought to have communication, both of the head with the members and of the members among themselves, as it is said in 1 Cor. 12:24, the members are anxious for one another, and if one member suffers something, all the members do likewise. But the just dead are members of this body, seeing that they are gathered with us and with God in faith, hope and charity. This is why St. Augustine (*de civitate Dei*, lib. 20 c. 9) says: "The souls of the faithful departed are not separated from the Church, which is the kingdom of Christ." Consequently, they may and must help the dead just as members of the same body.

Besides, Christ, because he is the head, benefitted the living while he was alive on earth, when dead he benefitted the dead, when living he benefitted the dead, and while he was dead he benefited the living. Therefore, it is also fitting that the members should so act among themselves so that just men who are alive would help the living, the dead would help the dead, the living the dead and the dead benefit the living. *First of all*, that Christ, while he was alive, benefitted the living is clear because he remitted the sins of the Magdalen (Luke 7:48), the Paralytic (Matthew 9:6), Zachaeus (Luke 19:9), Peter (Luke 22:61), of the thief: (Luke 23:43) and he took care of a great many corporally, as it is said in Mark 1:34, Acts 10:38 and other passages. That when dead he benefited the dead is clear; for descending to hell, he freed a great many from the sorrows of hell, as it says in Acts 2:24 and at the same time opened the tombs and roused a great many bodies of the Saints (Matthew 27:52). It is also certain that as a living man he benefited the dead: for the girl in the house of Jairus, the youth on the road and Lazarus in the tomb, were all dead and he recalled them to life (Matthew 9:25; Luke 7:15; John 11:44). Lastly, as a dead man he helped the living, for in his death he brought eternal life to us and now always fights for us in heaven, and has made himself our advocate (Hebrews 7;25; 1 John 2:1).

Thirdly and lastly, it is proven from the four divisions of members; three are certainly manifest, so the fourth should have place. Nobody denies that the living are helped by the living, since we see that some men are taught, instructed and fed by the word and the Sacraments

Ch. XV: The Suffrage of he Church benefits the dead 215

by others, and James 5:16 says: "Pray for each other that you might be saved."

Now it is certain that the dead benefit the dead: for Elisha, when he was dead, raised another man from the dead (4 Kings 13:21), and Abraham, when he was dead, received Lazarus into his bosom (Luke 16:22). Nor should there be any doubt whether the souls of the dead saints reigning with Christ should pray for the souls of the saints laboring in Purgatory. Domingo de Soto asserts the contrary (lib. 4 sent., dist. 45, quaest. 3 art. 2), and rashly, for apart from Peter the Cluniac (*loc. cit.*) St. Augustine says for this purpose it benefits the dead to be buried in the basilica of a martyr, so that one will be mindful of the dead man and at the same time remember the Martyr and commend the soul of the dead man to his prayers. And the whole Church begs God in the prayer: *Deus veniae largitor*,[14] etc. that by the suffrage of the Blessed Virgin and all the saints, all the faithful departed might hasten to attain a share of perpetual beatitude.

Moreover, that the dead can benefit the living is clear, for in 2 Maccabees 15:12-14, we read that Onias and

---

[14] Translator's note: This is an ancient prayer from the Office of the Dead at Lauds. *Deus veniae largitor, et humanae salutis amator, quaesumus clementiam tuam: ut nostrae congregationis fratres, propinquos, et benefactores, qui ex hoc saeculo transierunt, beata Maria semper virgine intercedente cum omnibus Sanctis tuis, ad perpetuae beatitudinis consortium pervenire concedas.*
"O God the bestower of forgiveness, and lover of human salvation, we beseech your mercy that you would permit the brethren of our congregation, relations and benefactors that departed from this world to come to the consort of human beatitude by the intercession of the Blessed and ever Virgin Mary, with all your saints."

Jeremiah were already long dead and were seen to pray for the people of the Jews that were still alive. Furthermore, the benefits shown by dead saints to men living here are innumerable and most certain. See St. Augustine (lib. 22 *de civitate Dei*, cap. 8) and Theodoret (*de Martyribus*). It is not unbelievable that even the souls of Purgatory pray for us and obtain things for us, seeing that the soul of Paschasius and St. Severinus worked miracles, even though they abided in Purgatory, as is clear from Gregory (*Dialog.* lib,. 4, cap. 40) and Peter Damian in his epistle on the miracles of his time.

Although St. Thomas teaches the contrary (2.2. qu. 83, art. 11 ad 3), still his reason does not convict the matter, for if those souls do not pray for us, there is either a cause, because they do not see God, or because they are in the greatest torments, or because they are inferior to us, but none of these can be said. Not the first, because in the time of the Old Testament, dead saints prayed for the living, as is clear from 2 Maccabees 31:121-14, although they did not yet see God.

Not the second, because the rich man in hell prayed for his brothers (Luke 16:27) although still he was in greater torments than the souls in Purgatory. Besides, martyrs are constituted in this world amid torments, but they prayed for themselves and others as is clear from St. Stephen (Acts 7:59). Likewise, suffering does not disturb souls in any mode of rational judgment, nor impede the good affect of the will; this happens to us by reason of corporal organs, which they lack. Lastly, there does not seem to be any uncertainty whether they might pray for themselves, torments not withstanding.

Ch. XV: The Suffrage of he Church benefits the dead 217

Not the third, because in this world we pray for Bishops and the Supreme Pontiffs who are our superiors and we also pray for those whom we do not doubt are holier than we are, just as Christians once prayed for the Apostle Paul when he sought their prayers (Romans 15:30).

Besides, even if the souls of Purgatory were inferior to us by reason of the punishments, still they are our superiors by reason of the grace and charity in which they are confirmed. But prayer which proceeds from charity. This is especially requires a superiority if it requires anything, therefore it is probable that they pray for us. But although these things are true, nevertheless it seems superfluous to beseech them to pray for us regularly because they cannot ordinarily recognize what we are doing in particular, rather they only know in general that we live in many dangers just as we only know in general that they are exceedingly tortured. St. Augustine shows that they are not concerned with our affairs, nor do they see our prayers in God, since they are not blessed, nor does it have the appearance of truth that what we are doing or ask is ordinarily revealed to them. So, if the living benefit the living, the dead benefit the dead, and the dead benefit the living, why couldn't the living benefit the dead?

Thus, it remains to answer the arguments which remain, apart from those we dealt with in the first and second question.

1) *The first argument.* Sirach 9:5, "Living they know they are going to die, but the dead know nothing more nor do they have anything beyond their reward, etc., nor a share in this life in the work which is done under the sun."

I respond: Wisdom speaks about the goods of this life and means to say the dead do not know how the affairs which remain here pass, nor can they use their own action, such as eating, drinking, giving alms, etc. Thus, it follows: "Go and eat in joy." Still, it is not concluded whether we can help them.

2) Calvin objects in the preface of the *Institutes*, first citing St. Ambrose: "We teach that we ought no longer to cling to the dead, rather it is enough to perform our duty and leave them" (*de Abraham*, lib. 1 cap. 7) and then he adds: "They burst through these limits when they maintain perpetual solicitude for the dead."

I respond: Here Ambrose argues about the mourning and pomp of funerals which he rightly willed to be moderated, but he does not forbid the solicitude of prayer for the dead, as is clear from the prayer of Ambrose himself on the death of Valentinian the younger. In the end, addressing Gratianus and Valentinian who were dead, he says: "Be blessed together, if my prayers have any strength, no day will pass you by in silence, no night shall pass without some portion given to my prayers; I will celebrate you in all offerings."

3) They object with St. Jerome, who while commenting in chapter 6 to the Galatians, explaining the verse: "Bear each other's burdens", says: "We are taught by this little sentence a new doctrine which was hidden; while we are in the present life, whether by prayer or council we can help each other; but when we come before the tribunal of Christ, not Job, not Daniel, not even Noah can pray for anyone, but each will bear his own burden." But this sentence of Jerome seems to be approved by the Church, nay more it is in the decretal of Gratian can. *In praesenti*, 13, q. 2, as has already been related.

I respond: Jerome spoke about those who sin mortally and die without penance, as Gratian annotated. Or, it must be said that Jerome spoke on the *last judgment*, when Purgatory will cease and suffrage will also cease, and only the final sentence of the judge will be entrusted to execution. That Jerome must be so understood is clear from that book against Vigilantius, where he accuses Vigilantius in earnest because he had said we can pray for each other while we live, but after death it is for no one to listen to a prayer of another.

4) From reason: It is better to make satisfaction by one's self than by another, since he will be less happy who makes satisfaction through another instead of himself, therefore, we ought not to pray for the dead lest we diminish their glory.

I respond: In this life it is better to make satisfaction by ourselves than through another, because while we make satisfaction we merit an increase of grace and glory at the same time; but in Purgatory, where souls cannot merit, it is not better to make satisfaction by one's self than though another.

5) We do not know, they say, where our dead are, and often while we think they are in Purgatory, they are in hell, or in heaven, therefore we pray in vain.

St. Augustine responds to this in *de cura*, that it is better that suffrage were superfluous for those who do not need it than that it should be lacking to those who need it, just as we do good to the unjust in this world lest the just be passed over. Additionally, a good work is never in vain, for it is meritorious to the one that does it, even if it confers no benefit on the one for whom it was done.

6) The justice of God renders evil for evil and good for good, but no man suffers for the sin of another, because a father will not carry the iniquity of the son (Ezechiel 18:20). Consequently, nobody ought to enjoy someone else's goods.

I respond: No man can be punished for the sin of another, *unless he becomes a partaker of the same sin*, either by consent or imitation. Exodus 20:5 speaks about such things when God punishes the sins of the Fathers in the sons to the third and fourth generation, which is understood when the sons imitate the parents, as the Church Fathers explain (Jerome, in cap. 18 of Ezechiel; Augustine, in Psalm 108; Chrysostom, homil. 29 in Gen., and Gregory, lib,. 25 moral. cap. 22). As a result, it is not absurd that someone enjoys the goods of another, if *with the consent of both and it is done willingly*, as in this place. The souls of Purgatory desire to be assisted and we wish to help them. Besides, to punish one for another is an injustice, and to receive the goods of one for another is mercy and liberality.

CHAPTER XVI
How many Kinds of Suffrage are there?

OW to the second, there are three types of suffrage: The Sacrifice of Mass, Prayer and any penitential works you like, and satisfactory works, such as almsgiving, fasting, pilgrimages and like things. Hence, we distinguish prayer from satisfactory works, although it might itself be satisfactory, because prayer helps the souls of the faithful departed in two ways; 1) as a certain punitive and laborious work, and in this mode it could be embraced under a satisfactory work; 2) in another mode it assists, as it is a mode of entreaty which is proper to prayer itself; in this way even the prayers of the Blessed benefit us and the souls in Purgatory, although they are not satisfactory.

For this purpose the dead are also assisted by indulgences, but these do not constitute a fourth kind of suffrage, because an indulgence is nothing other than the application of satisfactory or punitive works of Christ, and of the Saints to the dead. This is why it is said that an indulgence is "conceded" to the dead *by the mode of suffrage*, not by the mode of absolution; for the Pope cannot absolve the dead from penalties in the way he absolves the living because they are not subject to him. Nevertheless, he can, as supreme dispenser of the treasury of the Church, communicate to them good punitive works which are in the treasury, but we are going to speak on this matter elsewhere. In the meantime, see Cajetan in the first volume of the *opuscula*, tract. 16, q. 5 & 6.

That these are so is clear from the testimonies of the Fathers. St. Ambrose speaks about sacrifice and prayer for the dead in book 2, epist. 8 *ad Faustinum* on the death of his sister: "I think she is not to be wept over as much as to be pursued with prayers, nor mourned with your tears, rather, her soul must be commended to the Lord with prayers." Moreover, he treats on almsgiving in book 2 *de fide resurrectionis* in regard to the excess of his brother Satyrus, he exhorts parents to transmit a portion of the inheritance, which pertains to dead sons, to their spirits by giving alms to the poor.

St. Augustine, in sermon 32, speaks about the words of the Apostle: "With the prayers of the holy Church and the salutary sacrifice, as well as almsgiving, there is no doubt the dead receive assistance."

Chrysostom (hom. 69 *ad populum*), says: "The commemoration of the dead that is made in the awesome mysteries was not rashly ratified by the Apostles, for from it they obtain much fruit and profit." He says the same thing in homily 41 on 1 Corinthians: "The dead man is not helped by tears but prayers, supplications and almsgiving."

Add to these the testimony of the angel cited by Bede (*histor.* lib. 5, cap. 13), "The prayers of the living, almsgiving, fasting, and especially the celebration of the Mass brings assistance so that they might be freed before the day of judgment."

Here there is only one doubt: Would restitution of someone else's goods benefit the dead, and hence a fourth kind of suffrage? For souls are often said to appear and ask that restitution be made for them of those things which they either forgot about or could not restore. St. Brigit, in book 6 of her revelations, chapter 66, affirms that souls are tortured until something that was taken by them unjustly is restored.

Domingo de Soto responds (4 dist. 45 quaest. 2 art. 3) that restitution of this sort does not assist the dead if it is made and it does not hinder them if it is not. God does not punish except for someone's own sin contracted in this life; so either the dead man sinned by failing to make restitution, or did not sin. If he did not sin, then he could have, or did, possess a thing in good faith, thus, he ought not also be punished; if he sinned, he will be punished for the sin of negligence for that matter in Purgatory, but after he has undergone due punishment, he will be saved whether the thing is restored or not. He has already been rendered powerless to make restitution, nor ought his salvation depend upon the will of another, otherwise the soul could remain in Purgatory for ever if an heir were never to make restitution; this is why, if restitution could be made and was not, by the negligence of the heir, the heir will indeed sin, but it will not harm that soul; if it is done it confers no benefit to that soul because the restitution is not satisfaction for sin, for satisfaction is a good penal work, but it is penal to give one's own things, not to restore someone else's.

I respond to those apparitions: Perhaps the souls did not ask for restitution *as restitution*, but *as almsgiving*, although it does not benefit the soul if one would restore someone else's goods, which he is held to restore. Nevertheless, it may rightly benefit if restitution of something else was made which one is not held to; for that is a certain almsgiving and hence satisfactory.

CHAPTER XVII
Who can Assist Souls

O the third: who can assist souls with their suffrage? A just man. An unjust man cannot make satisfaction for himself, let alone for others.

But someone will say: Isn't the Mass of a bad priest beneficial to the dead? Isn't also a just master that commands almsgiving to be made from his possessions for the dead, but then they are given by an unjust minister, still beneficial to the soul for whom they were given? *I respond:* it does benefit the soul, but in these cases it is not the unjust minister who causes the benefit, but rather the just master.

But again, someone will say: "What if a just prelate commands his spiritual sons to pray or fast for the dead, and these sons are unjust?

Paludanus (4 sent. dist. 45, qu. 1) answers that all these benefit. But de Soto is more correct to deny it (*ibid.* q. 2 art. 2). For when a servant gives alms from his master's money, that work is properly of his master, not of the servant, and therefore, the malice of the minister does not spoil the work; but when the one in obedience prays or fasts, it is properly the work of that subject, for he acts with his own labor, not the labor of his master. For the same reason, St. Jerome says that it is better to give alms to a poor just man than an unjust poor man, because the former, praying for a benefactor, is heard while the other is not.

CHAPTER XVIII
Who Benefits from Suffrage?

O the fourth, it is certain that the suffrage of the Church benefits neither the blessed nor the damned, but only those who abide in Purgatory. The first do not need it, the second cannot be helped by it, as all the Scholastics teach (4 dist. 45) following Augustine, who, in the *Enchiridion* (cap. 110) and *De cura pro mortuis* (cap. 1) says that the suffrage of the Church is a thanksgiving for the very good, propitiation for the very wicked, and for the very wicked it is of no assistance, but such as it is a consolation to the living.

But there are three difficulties to the contrary. *First,* on the blessed. It seems false that the suffrage does not benefit the blessed, for Epiphanius (*haer.* 75) and Cyril (*Catech.* 5 *Mystagogica*) as well as the liturgy of St. John Chrysostom say sacrifice is offered to God for the Apostles, Martyrs, Prophets, etc.

Secondly, the Church often reads in her prayers: "We have received the holy mysteries, O Lord, which, as they benefit thy saints in glory, so we ask that they may benefit us like a healing remedy." And in ancient missals, as Innocent III relates (cap. *Cum Marthae, extra de Celebratione Missarum, in die 8 Leonis,* it is said: "We annually beseech thee, O Lord, that this sacrifice might benefit the soul of St. Leo." And although this prayer was changed, still we say in the secret prayer for the same feast: "May the annual solemnity of St. Leo, thy confessor and Pontiff render us acceptable so that by these duties of pious reconciliation, a blessed reward might accompany it and acquire the gifts of thy grace for us."

Besides, Chrysostom also says (hom. 33 in Matth.), exhorting men to give alms for their dead sons: "You think he is pure from sin? Give his possessions to others that he might cleanse himself of those stains; do you think he died in justice? Offer your own for him to increase the reward and payment."

The response to the *first* is easy: That something is sacrificed for the saints is not so that we might ask something for them, but so that we might give thanks to God for the glory he has conferred on them; for it is what St. Augustine says, thanksgiving is made for the very good.

Pope Innocent responds to the rest, as above, in a two-fold manner: a) when the Church seeks glory for the saints who possess the kingdom of heaven, it does not ask that they would increase in glory, but that their glory would increase among us, *i.e.* that their glory would be made known to the whole world, and they would be glorified everywhere more and more; b) he says it does not seem absurd if we ask for an increase of something *accidental* to their glory; c) add thirdly, perhaps glory of the body is sought, which they will have on the day of the resurrection; for even if that glory were obtained for certain, which is due for their merits, still it is not absurd for them to desire this, and ask so that it would be due in many modes. So, when Augustine says (sermon. 17) from the words of the Apostle that it does a martyr injury to pray for him, it is understood on those who are prayed to as Martyrs for the remission of sin or essential glory, as if they lacked it.

Ch. XVIII: Who benefits from suffrage?

The *second* difficulty is on the damned. For Augustine says, "But those who benefit from suffrage either do so for this purpose, so that a full remission is made, or the damnation itself becomes more tolerable" (*Enchir.* cap. 110). And in chapter 112, he so speaks: "Let them think the punishments of the damned are mitigated, little by little, for certain intervals of time, if it gives them pleasure to think so, provided it is understood that they remain in the wrath of God, this is, damnation itself."

Chrysostom said the same thing (hom. 3 in *ep. ad Philipp.*), after he had said prayer must be made for the dead, he added: "That indeed is true what we have said, because they have departed in faith; but it seems catechumens are not worthy of this consolation, but are destitute of all help except one alone. But what? It is permitted to give alms on their behalf, from where they will obtain some rest."

Besides, Damascene, in his prayer on the dead, not only relates that story about Trajan and Falconilla freed from hell by the prayer of Gregory and Thecla, which we related above, but he also adds from the history of Palladius ad Lausum, that St. Macharius at some time asked the dry skull of a certain idolater whether the prayers of the living were of any benefit to the dead, the skull gave this response: "When you offer prayers for the dead, we perceive some alleviation."

Besides, Prudentius says, in his hymn for the new light at the Easter Vigil:

*Sunt et spiritibus saepe nocentibus,
pœnarum celebres sub styge feriae, etc.*[15]

Then, Innocent III, cap. *Cum Marthae*, places a fourfold division; for he says from the dead there were some that were very good who do not need suffrage, certain ones men that were very bad, who cannot be helped, some men only somewhat good, whom suffrage benefits to expiation; and certain men only somewhat bad whom they benefit to propitiation—but certainly the last member does not seem to fit, except for the children in limbo. For, if the very good are in heaven, the very wicked are in the fires of hell; therefore, the somewhat good are in Purgatory, but wherever will the somewhat bad go, apart from limbo? Therefore, suffrage will benefit although they are still not in purgatory.

I respond to the *first*: Augustine understood by a more tolerable damnation, a mitigation of the punishments of Purgatory, as is clear from the preceding three-member division.

I say to the *second*, there Augustine does not argue on prayer for the dead, but only to say that it is not conceded to be erroneous that the damned would be punished short of what they ought; he teaches this more clearly in book 21, *de Civitate Dei*, cap. 24.

To the *third*: Chrysostom seems to only deny one must pray *publicly* or offer sacrifice for Catechumens, just as the Council of Braga defined at a different time (I. can. 35).

---

[15] Translator's note: "There are also festivals for wicked spirits, famous for their crimes in the underworld, etc." *Cathemer. Hymn v* (lin. 125).

Ch. XVIII: Who benefits from suffrage?

To the *fourth*, St. Thomas in 4 dist. 45, art. 2 q. 2, after refuting some inept answers of Praepositivus, Porretanus and others, answers that the souls of the damned do not perceive some true mitigation of their punishments by the prayers of the saints, but only some inane and fallacious joy, which seems to be in respect to their associates in punishments, such as the joy of demons, when they deceive someone. But perhaps it would be better rejected as false and apocryphal, which is asserted about that skull, for such a thing is not found in the book of Palladius, nor does it have the appearance of truth that St. Macharius prayed for dead unbelievers.

To the *fifth*, I say it is nothing other than the poetic license of Prudentius.

To the *last*, which usually tortures many, I suspect Innocent III had a lapse of memory in the division, which is cited by Augustine three-fold, as four-fold, for with Augustine the moderately good and moderately bad are the same. Moreover, Innocent distinguishes this member into two, saying: "Some are moderately good, others moderately bad." Still, we can say the moderately good are said to be those who have no sin but still have to undergo punishment, while the moderately bad are said to be those who have some sin but it is only venial.

The *third* difficulty is on the souls of Purgatory. Theologians agree on two things, and do not on one. 1) They agree that all suffrage benefits everyone, at least *insofar as they convey a new joy*, as that is common to every good work, that all good men rejoice in it according to that of Psalm 118 (119): 63, "I am a partaker of all that fear you."

2) They agree that common suffrage which is made for all the dead, also benefits all the souls of Purgatory; not only by reason of joy, but also by reason of satisfaction, for there is no reason why someone would be excluded.

3) But they disagree in regard to particular suffrages. For Cajetan (tomus 1 *opusc.* tract. 16 q. 5) teaches that all souls may and must be assisted by common suffrage; yet, in regard to particular suffrage which is made for them, they do not help except for those which they merit personally so that such would benefit them. Moreover, he says these souls personally merit that had a special devotion to the keys of the Church here on earth and were solicitous for the souls of others, and he proves it from St. Augustine (*de cura pro mortuis*, c. 1; *Enchir.* cap. 109).

But others, whom St. Thomas cites in 4 dist. 45, q. 2 art. 4, say that the suffrage which is made for one, does not only benefit him alone, but also all others; no less others than him; just as a lamp enkindled for a master equally gives light to the servants who are in the same place.

The common opinion is in the mean, which is that one's own suffrage is beneficial to all and him individually by reason of satisfaction for which it is made. *To all*, against Cajetan, is clear, because the foundation of the communication of suffrage is not some peculiar merit, but the state of grace. St. Augustine, when he says suffrage is beneficial only to those that merit so that they could benefit themselves, by the excluding adjective *alone*, does not exclude any soul of Purgatory, but only damned souls. Moreover, it must be noted carefully that Augustine, in the *Enchiridion*, does not say that suffrage only helps the dead who personally merited it for their benefit, but anyone who merited for it for their benefit.

Ch. XVIII: Who benefits from suffrage? 231

This is why Cajetan, who says all souls can be assisted but *de facto* are not helped, does not follow Augustine as he supposed. That these particular suffrages are beneficial only to those for whom they are made is certain; for the application of goods of this sort depends upon the intention of the one applying it, nor ought these suffrages be compared to the light of a lamp, but rather to the money which is paid by one man for another.

I also highlight that passage of Augustine favoring this teaching from the *de cura pro mortuis*, c. 4, where he says that the Church prays for all the dead in general so that those who are destitute of parents or friends to pray for them and would otherwise be destitute of help shall at least have the help from their common mother, which is the Church.

CHAPTER XIX
On Funerals

E have spoken hitherto on the spirits of the dead; now we must address the burial of their bodies. The heretics of this time do not rebuke the burial itself, rather the many things surrounding burial.

Firstly, that we bury them in sacred places, and also that we raise cemeteries for this purpose. Some of the heretics rebuke this, such as in Bohemia (as Aeneas Sylvius cites, *de origine Boemorum*, cap. 35). Furthermore, the argument can be made that the place of burial is of no benefit from the words of Luke 12:4, "Do not fear those who kill the body, and after this have no more power to do anything." Likewise, from cap. *Sacris, extra de sepulturis*, where it is said that it is no judgment against a man if he is buried in a vile place, or in no place at all. Likewise, from St. Augustine (*de Civitate Dei* lib. 1, c. 12; *de cura mortuis*), where he says that burial and the pomp of a funeral is a comfort for the living but no assistance for the dead.

Secondly, they rebuke the use of candles. And because in the Council of Elibertinus, can. 34, it was stated that candles were not to be lit in the cemeteries on the day of death, as the fathers of that Council said: "The spirits of the dead must not be disturbed."

Thirdly, they rebuke anniversaries and so many repetitions of the funeral on the third, seventh and thirtieth day because it is a sign that faith is wanting to repeat the same prayers to many times. In addition, because St. Ambrose (*de Abraham*, lib. 1 cap. 9), while speaking about Genesis 23:3, that Abraham rose from the office of the funeral, "We teach that we ought no longer cling to the dead, rather it is enough to perform our duty and leave them." Calvin, explaining such a passage in the preface of the *Institutes*, says that those who do not cease praying for the dead are rebuked by that passage.

Fourthly, they rebuke the fact that we regard burial as a meritorious work as well as pleasing to God, since no such command as this is found from God. In fact, while the Lord enumerated the works of mercy in Matthew 25, he did not mention burial.

These not withstanding, we assert that burial is a good and useful thing, and all the rites of the Church for burying the dead are ancient as well as holy.

The fact that the matter is good and meritorious is proven from that of 2 Kings 2:5, "Ye blessed of the Lord, who have shown this mercy with your master, Saul, and buried him, and now the Lord will reward you." In Tobit 12:12, among the works of Tobit, the angel extols that he buried the dead. In Matthew 26:10-12, "She has done good to me, ... for by this anointing she has prepared me for burial."

That it is ancient and useful can easily be shown, for everything which we now preserve in the Church was always in her use. First, the bodies are now washed; that was also done as is clear from Acts 9:37 with Tabitha, and is cited by Gregory (*Dial.* lib. 3, cap. 17; lib. 4, cap. 16 & 27).

Secondly, bodies were buried with honor and brought to the tomb with many attendants. We read that this was so done in Genesis 50:7, Luke 7:12 as well as with Gregory Nazianzen (orat. 2 *in Julianum*), Sulpitius (*vita S. Martini*), Jerome (*vita S. Fabiolae, S. Paulae*) and others.

Thirdly, the bodies of the faithful are buried in churches and sacred places; so also Jacob and Joseph the Patriarchs who died in Egypt wished to be buried in the promised land, in which the temple was going to be built and Christ was going to be born (Genesis 49:29; 50:24). Then, in the times of Christians, many witness that the bodies of the faithful were buried in Churches (Ambrose, *de Abraham*, lib. 1, c. 9; Jerome, *vita Paulae, et Fabiolae*; Gregory *Dialog.* lib. 3, c. 13; Augustine, *de cura pro mortuis,* cap. 1).

Fourthly, the bodies of the faithful are buried with the chant of hymns and Psalms, and this is also witnessed by Gregory Nazianzen (*loc. cit.*), Chrysostom (hom. 4 in Hebr.) Jerome (*loc. cit.*) Suplpitius (*vita S. Martini*) and the most ancient of all, Dionysius the Aeropagate, *de Ecclesiastica hierarchia*, cap. 7).[16]

Fifthly, the use of lamps and lit candles at a funeral was done then as now. Gregory of Nyssa (epist. ad Olympia on the death of her sister), Gregory Nazianzen and Chrysostom (*ll.cc.*), Jerome (*loc. cit.*) and Theodoret (*hist.* lib. 5 cap. 36) as well as others.

Sixthly, the sacrifice of the alter is offered for them. So it was also done formerly as Tertullian witnesses (*de corona militis*) Cyprian (lib. 1, epistl. 9), Augustine (*Confessiones*, lib. 9 c. 12), Ambrose (*oratione de Valentiniani obitu*) and others.

Seventhly, Mass is offered and they are prayed for not only when they are buried, but also on the anniversary of

---

[16] Translator's note: Although modern scholarship questions the attribution to Dionysius, the matter was not in doubt with Bellarmine or with the Protestants of his day.

their death, as is clear from Tertullian (*de Monogamia*), and Gregory Naianzen (*oratione in Caesarium fratrem*).

Eighth, not only on the anniversary, but also on the third, seventh and thirtieth day, as Ambrose shows in the beginning of his *oration for the death of Theodosius*, and this is preserved even today.

Ninth, tombstones are raised up; the same was once done in Genesis 35:20, Acts 2:29, 1 Maccabees 13:27).

Now, what the advantage of this might be is a little more obscure. In the first place two errors must be rejected, which St. Augustine rejects (*de cura pro mortuis*, c.2). 1) What the pagans thought, that burial was necessary for souls to be able to rest, according to the fables of Virgil (*Aeneidos*, lib. 6). 2) The other is of those who thought that some sense is still present in the bodies of the dead.

Now that these two errors have been rejected, we say that burial is useful both for the living and the dead. For the living in four ways. 1) *First*, to ward off the stench and horror of cadavers by burial, which would do no little harm to the living.

2) *Second*, for the living to witness their faith in the resurrection and the immortality of the soul by such zeal. We would not take such care of the bodies of the dead unless we thought they will rise again. Nor would we light candles unless we meant to show that souls live after the death of their bodies.

3) *Third*, for the living to be warned of their own death, this is why the tombs of the dead are called monuments.[17]

---

[17] Translator's note: There is a symmetry in the Latin that is lost here; the word used here for warn is *admonere*, the participle for which is *admonitus*, from which *monimenta* (monument) comes.

4) *Fourth*, by that office the living make satisfaction in some way for the affections they hold for the dead. If we carefully arrange the garments and rings of friends, certainly much more their bodies; and this is what St. Augustine means when he says that the pomp of burial is a comfort for the living.

Now we add the utility from burial for the dead, and this is also fourfold. 1) *First*, that the honor paid to them remains in the minds of the living, for one cannot lack some ignominy when the foulness of our bodies is exposed to the sight of the living. Further, it is judged no small punishment when someone is deprived of burial by a judge and commanded to be hung from a gibbet or a wheel to be food for the birds.

2) *Second*, that it satisfies the desires they had while they were alive, for there is no one that hates his own flesh, as it is said in Ephesians 5:29, and thus while anyone lives, he desires also that after his death his body will be handled with integrity; nay more, it is believable that souls, once they have been freed from their bodies, even if they did not know what happened to their bodies, still would desire they be held with integrity, just as they also desire to go back to them as Augustine teaches (*de Genes. ad literam*, lib. 12, cap. 35) and hence we see the disobedient prophet was given as a punishment that he would not be buried with his fathers (3 Kings 13:24).

3) *The third utility* arises from the fact that many carry them to burial; hence it happens *per accidens* that many will also pray for them.

4) *The fourth* is taken from the fact that they are buried in the Churches of saints; from there it happens that when their friends remember them they will also remember the

saint in whose Church they are buried at the same time and will frequently commend them to his patronage. St. Augustine posits this advantage in his work *de cura pro mortuis*, cap. 4 & 5, and St. Gregory (in *Dialog.* lib. 4 cap. 50).

From all these we make our responses to the arguments. I say *to the first*, with Augustine (*de Civitate Dei* lib. 1 cap. 12), that the Lord speaks on the pain with which bodies are afflicted while they live. Then in verse 4 he says: "After this they have no more to do," because the dead body, if it were cut or mutilated or burned clearly does not sense the pain. Nevertheless, it does not follow that some almsgiving should not be made to satisfy the desire that the man had while he lived, and perhaps still has to bury his body. I say *to the second*, the Pope speaks in that decretal on the advantage to *eternal salvation*, and teaches that burial does not benefit *per se*, nor does it cause any harm to attaining eternal salvation *per se*, as we said by reason of the prayers of friends. I say to the *third*, Augustine only teaches that burial *per se* offers no aid to the dead so they would attain eternal life, but comfort to the living; nevertheless, it benefits them *per accidens* as he himself teaches in the same book.

To that other citation from the Council of Elibertinus, I respond that in that Council ceremony is rebuked and forbidden because it was done from the superstition of the gentiles who thought dead bodies sensed something; but after that error was put to rest the same ceremony was used for another end, namely to show that souls live and even the body was going to rise again in its time, and our dead are sons of light, not of darkness. Furthermore, what that Council says, that the spirits of the dead must not be disturbed does not mean those spirits are really restless, but to dispel the people of an error of this sort, just as Ambrose says in the aforementioned epistle (lib. 2 epist. 8) that his correspondent should not mourn his dead sister with tears, but prayers.

I say to the third that it is not a sign that faith is wanting, rather a sign of longing and fervor to repeat the same prayers, for Paul does the very thing in 2 Corinthians 12:8 when he "asked the Lord three times," and the Lord himself repeated the same prayer three times in Matthew 26:44.

We respond to the citation from Ambrose as above in chapter 15, he is not talking about prayers but about weeping and sorrow; for he says the same thing in the oration on the death of Valentinian: "Blessed together, if my prayers have any strength, no day will pass by you in silence, no night composed without some portion given to my prayers; I will celebrate you in all offerings."

To the *last*, I respond from chapter 25 of Matthew. Firstly, when Chrysostom says in homil. 84 on John that the Lord did not add "I was dead and you buried me," because men usually not only give this alms of their own will, but also are given to too much excess in so doing; for just as in other good things, so also here a certain abuse mixed itself in, whereby rich men customarily are buried clothed in precious garments; it would be better and much more pleasing and useful for the dead, as Chrysostom says in the same place, for the precious garments to be given to the poor for the soul of the man that is buried. Thus the Lord, not only to correct an abuse, but even more, because it did not seem necessary to commend this duty too much, did not number this almsgiving with the rest.

Secondly, it can be said that the Lord did not call to mind this almsgiving because it was the least and most obscure of all, as St. Augustine teaches (*de cura pro mortuis*, cap. 3), for the Lord meant to show that he justly rewards the good and punishes the wicked, and therefore he only called to mind those works which evidently, and in the judgment of all, are works of mercy. And this will suffice for this whole disputation.

END OF THE THIRD GENERAL CONTROVERSY

LAUS DEO, VIRGINIQUE MATRI MARIÆ

THE COLLECTED WORKS OF ST. ROBERT BELLARMINE

The 'De Controversiis'

Published:
On the Roman Pontiff
On Councils
On the Church Militant
On the Marks of the Church
On Purgatory

Forthcoming:
On Clergy, Monks, Laity
On Beatification and Canonization of the Saints
On Relics and Images
On the Sacraments
On Grace, Justification and Free Will
On Good Works
On Indulgences
On the Word of God
On Christ

Alia:
Autobiography
Catechism

To assist the work of translating all of St. Robert Bellarmine, purchase these and other great titles or consider making a donation!
http://www.mediatrixpress.com

www.ingramcontent.com/pod-product-compliance
Lightning Source LLC
Chambersburg PA
CBHW011129070526
44583CB00023B/2962